How to Protect Your Children

on the Internet

How to Protect Your Children
on the Internet

A Road Map for Parents and Teachers

GREGORY S. SMITH

Westport, Connecticut
London

Library of Congress Cataloging-in-Publication Data

Smith, Gregory S., 1963–
    How to protect your children on the Internet : a roadmap for parents and teachers /
Gregory S. Smith.
        p. cm.
    Includes bibliographical references and index.
    ISBN 978-0-275-99472-3 (alk. paper)
    1. Internet and children.   2. Technology and children.   3. Internet—Safety
measures.   4. Safety education.   I. Title.
    HQ784.I58S65   2007
    305.235—dc22   2007016348

British Library Cataloguing in Publication Data is available.

Library of Congress Catalog Card Number: 2007016348
ISBN-13: 978-0-275-99472-3
ISBN-10: 0-275-99472-4

First published in 2007

Praeger Publishers, 88 Post Road West, Westport, CT 06881
An imprint of Greenwood Publishing Group, Inc.
www.praeger.com

Printed in the United States of America

The paper used in this book complies with the
Permanent Paper Standard issued by the National
Information Standards Organization (Z39.48–1984).

10 9 8 7 6 5 4 3 2 1

To all parents and children who have been harmed, duped, or deceived via the Internet. Also, for all of the hard-working law enforcement, child therapists, parents, teachers, and Internet security professionals dedicating their time and effort to protecting children.

This book is intended for parents with children between the age of 8 and 17 who have access to the Internet and the educators that teach them. The Internet and technologies that enable online interaction and access to a variety of content can be a perilous place for minors. The dangers are real, and parents today are confronted with many threats that they simply don't understand. Simply stated, the purpose of this book is to share the risks of the Internet via exposing some recent real-world tragedies, while providing a pragmatic approach and road map to help parents protect their children against the threats of going online.

Contents

Preface

I am an international expert in the field of information technology and the parent of two children. Like many other parents, I walk a fine line of analyzing and determining just how much technology freedom to give my kids. The Internet is an abundant resource of interconnected networks, servers, and, yes, content that with the advent of World Wide Web and browser technology has transformed the way that people research, shop, conduct business, and communicate. That said, the Internet and online interaction technologies can be a perilous place for kids. The dangers are real, and parents are confronted with many threats that they may not fully grasp. The purpose of this book is to share the risks by describing some recent real tragedies and hidden secrets of online activities, while providing a pragmatic approach and plan to help parents protect their children against the threats of going online.

THE NEED

Parents today with children ranging from the age of 8 to 17 are often somewhat clueless about the real risks when their children access the Internet via a variety of devices and applications such as (1) email, (2) instant messaging (IM), (3) browsing, (4) blogs, (5) cell phones with text messaging, (6) personal digital assistant (PDA) devices, (7) online chat, and (8) social networking sites (such as MySpace). More and more youths today around the world are going online and engaging in activities that are quite risky, such as viewing mature and adult content and being exposed to predators that use the Internet to target minors for sex and other harmful intent. Many parents have read some of the horror stories printed in local and national newspapers or exposed by TV media such as NBC's *Dateline* about potential harm that can come to children online.

Most teenagers simply don't understand the risks of accessing the Internet and can be harmed greatly as a result of their naiveté. This book exposes the risks and provides a road map for parents to become more engaged in their children's online activities as well as techniques and tips to help protect their children. Kids today are using technology in ways that parents don't even know are going on, such as conducting private phone conversations over the Internet with friends and sometimes strangers. Voice technologies integrated with free instant messaging tools provide children with an opportunity to fly under the parental radar undetected, as there is no log of calls made or received.

As I write this, there are over 6 billion people in the world, and more than a billion have access to the Internet. The United States accounts for over 300 million people as of October 2006. According to the 2000 U. S. census, there are approximately 34.5 million households (32.8 percent) with children under the age of 18. Children at risk today between the ages of 5 and 19 years old comprise over 60 million of the total population estimated by the Census Bureau. The numbers speak for themselves and highlight the fact that millions of parents are challenged with the dilemma of how to protect their kids from online risks.

THE SOLUTION

How to Protect Your Children on the Internet brings to light some chilling examples of how minors and adults conduct themselves online and follows up with recommendations to mitigate the risks by a variety of online tools and countermeasures. Part One provides an introduction to the Internet with a highlight of the benefits and risks of going online. The bulk of this part of the book explains some key technologies and why they're important for parents and educators to understand, along with the risks associated with going online and what parents are doing to protect their children.

Part Two is designed to give parents and educators a map and clear set of recommendations on how to protect children if they use a variety of the Internet-enabled tools and technologies that introduce risk in the first place. These include email, IM, Internet browsing, blogs, cell phones with text messaging, PDAs, online chat, social networking sites, and even Internet-connected video cameras. The final chapter concludes with some helpful hints for parents to talk to their children about the risks associated with using the Internet.

TARGET AUDIENCE

This book is targeted primarily toward parents, most of whom are not aware of the real and potentially dangerous risks when their children connect to the Internet. The book provides parents with a computer technology primer to educate them about the tools that enable online activity and their associated risks and provides with a set of software solutions and recommendations to mitigate harmful risk to children. Parents in North America are the most connected to the Internet, with well over 50 percent of households going online in some form or another. Teenagers today are usually more sophisticated than their parents with regard to accessing and using online technologies. They are also getting smarter at hiding their methods for doing the wrong things online. Many other industrialized nations around the globe (in Asia, Europe, and South America) are going online more, and as a result, their children are being exposed to the good and bad portions of the Internet. Parents around the world with computers and other connected devices are exposing their children to risks in ways that they simply don't understand.

A secondary audience includes private and public school educators (K–12) as they attempt to guide and teach students the benefits and risks of the Internet. Technology permeates the K–12 educational environment, so risk is introduced. Many schools attempt to limit those risks with Internet filters and blocks, but many dangers persist. More technologies are using encryption to bypass sophisticated Internet filters and security software. By doing so, they can go virtually undetected. Examples include voice calls over the Internet (such as Skype), encrypted pornography sites, and IM tools that use common protocols and ports that change to allow users to browse the Internet. Unfortunately, there is no standard boilerplate at schools today and as a result, some have better technology to protect children than others.

APPROACH

The information presented in this book, along with recommendations, come from a variety of sources including research reports, case studies, child advocacy organizations and Web sites, interviews with experts, interviews and surveys involving parents with children that have access to the Internet, and my own experiences as both a parent and a technology professional with over 20 years of information technology experience as well as a decade in the classroom educating the next generation of IT leaders.

Acknowledgments

Over the past 20 years, I've had wonderful opportunities to learn, grow, and apply information technology (IT) best practices to businesses, deliver results for customers, and mentor and teach technical staff and graduate students craving more knowledge and best practices. I believe that it's the responsibility of today's leaders to give back to their community in one way or another. This book is one way for me to do just that—by sharing my knowledge and expertise in technology and education with an eye for helping millions of parents and teachers better protect their children from the risks associated with accessing the Internet. One specific person along the way taught me some of these leadership traits. I'd like to recognize Deborah Hechinger as a mentor and a role model. By her own actions, Debbie teaches others to do their best and to make a difference in life. My first interaction with her was in a professional nature, but that has clearly grown into a more trusted and true friendship. Thanks for being a great role model, Debbie!

Proofreading is an art form, often missed by an author who may be too close to his or her own work. I'd like to personally thank Catherine Golden and Anne Topp for their eyes on this project. Also, a special thanks goes out to Stan Wakefield, the literary agent who introduced me to the publishing team at the Greenwood Publishing Group. Thanks again!

Honest sounding boards are very important to me, especially in the development of a book as controversial and technically complex as this one. I'd like to thank two particular friends of mine, both initially via professional association, who supported my decision to write this manuscript with solid encouragement and subtle tones of friendship and were instrumental in getting the word out in the press. They are Martha Heller of the Z Resource Group and Eric Lundquist of *eWeek* magazine.

In closing, I pay special thanks to the wonderful folks at Praeger and the Greenwood Publishing Group, especially Suzanne Staszak-Silva for her efforts in making this book a world-class publication. Last and most important, I thank my family for their continued and generous support during the writing of this manuscript, and my parents, Josephine and Carl, for their never-ending encouragement to take risks and succeed. They've instilled a key motto for how I live my life—*never give up*!

PART ONE

Introduction to Technology and Risks on the Internet

One

Welcome to the Internet

Everything that you can imagine is real.

—Pablo Picasso

GROWING UP

Most parents today don't have a clue how to protect their children from the risks of using the Internet. In fact, most would probably admit that their teenagers know more about technology than they do—putting themselves at a disadvantage from the start. *Everything that you can imagine is real.* If Picasso were alive today, the reality of his words when applied to the Internet would blow him away. It's true—if you can think it, it can be built, packaged, and sold.

When I was a kid growing up in Flemington, New Jersey, we listened to rock and roll bands like KISS and Bruce Springsteen, rode our bikes, played sports, went to school, and checked out the opposite sex at school-sponsored dances and the mall. We didn't have online predators. We didn't have hard-core pornography accessible at the click of a mouse. We didn't have email accounts, text messaging, and caller ID. We didn't have instant messaging and definitely could not make private phone calls over the Internet without our parents' knowledge. Hell—we didn't even have phones in our bedrooms! Our parents were in complete control of our upbringing, and they liked it that way.

For the most part, parents today are clueless about computer technology and the Internet along with the risks. Simply put, adults are at a technological disadvantage when compared to teens and are confused on how to gain control again.

I know—I've spoken to many parents, and the topic of Internet risks comes up frequently. Within minutes into those types of conversations, I'm often asked for advice. My first tip: read this book cover to cover and pay clear attention to the recommendations section at the end of each chapter. Tip number 2: get up to speed on technology and regain control over your children. Tip number 3: don't be afraid to be a parent. Some parents I've spoken with are more interested in being their kid's best friend. It's important at times to play both roles, but parents should never lose sight of the fact that it is their obligation and responsibility to parent and protect their children. Those who bow to pressure from their kids, especially teenagers, and relax their responsibilities are potentially putting their children at risk. More important, if their children are harmed physically or emotionally as a result of going online and the parent has failed to provide protection, they are partly to blame for the tragedy. It's easy to knuckle under to pressure, especially from teens, but parents must be strong and take responsibility for properly raising their children. That includes learning when to say no to certain things in an effort to guarantee their safety.

When I was a teen, to access semi-nude and somewhat respectable photos of naked women, we had to get older kids to buy magazines such as *Penthouse* or *Playboy* for us. The biggest problem I ever had growing up was hiding a *Playboy* from my mother that a friend had given me for my fourteenth birthday, and even that didn't work out well. She found it under my mattress, gave me holy hell, and sent me to my room for the afternoon, where I waited for my father to address the issue when he came home from work. "Wait until your father gets home," she said to me with her index finger pointed at my face. I waited for hours in my room for my father to come home from work. I can still remember the sound of his footsteps coming up the stairs and walking down the hallway toward my room. He knocked on my bedroom door and then came in. After a brief pause, he said with a slight smile on his face, "Don't let your mother catch you with this again," and promptly walked out. Whew—all that worrying for nothing. If I could go back and do that decision over again, I'd probably hide the magazine under my parent's mattress—on my father's side.

I am an internationally recognized expert in the field of information technology. I'm also the parent of two children. Like many other parents, I walk a fine line of analyzing and determining just how much technology freedom to give my kids. The Internet is a wonderful and abundant resource of interconnected networks, servers, and, yes, content that with the advent of Web and browser technology has transformed the way that people research, shop, conduct business, and communicate. That said, the Internet and online communication technologies can be a perilous place for minors. The dangers are real, and parents are confronted with many threats they simply don't fully comprehend. At the end of each chapter, I provide clear and concise recommendations to parents and teachers. To begin Part Two of the book, the recommendations are broken down into three different age groups that mimic the typical school system environment and the social challenges that go along with each increasing age level. These three categories are:

- Category 1: Elementary School (ages 8–11).
- Category 2: Middle School (ages 12–14).
- Category 3: High School (ages 15–18).

Chances are good that most parents know a bit more about technology than their children while their kids are in the first category, elementary school. That lead usually erodes quickly as kids enter the socially awkward and more competitive environment of middle school, where technology is more often used in support of school projects and to keep up with the latest tween and teen fad. By the time most youths reach high school, they usually surpass their parents with knowledge of technology, especially if the parents are not involved in the technology or education profession. Teens in category 3 are at an age that effective monitoring, sometimes via stealth software, best comes into play as they may try to conceal their online activities.

Parents today with children, minors ranging from the age of 8 to 17, are at least moderately in the dark about the risks when their children access the Internet via a variety of devices and applications, such as email, instant messaging (IM), surfing or browsing, blogs, cell phones with text messaging, personal digital assistant (PDA) devices, chat rooms, and social networking sites. Youth around the world are going online more often and engaging in activities that are quite risky, such as viewing mature and adult content and being exposed to predators that use the Internet to target minors for sex and other harmful intent. Some have read some of the horror stories printed in local and national newspapers or exposed via TV media such as NBC *Dateline* about harm that can come to children that go online.

According to the 2000 U.S. census, there are slightly more than 281 million people living in the United States, with approximately 34.5 million households (32.8 percent) that have children under the age of 18.[1] Unofficially, the population total in the United States crossed the 300 million mark sometime in October 2006. Children at risk between the ages of 5 and 19 years old comprise over 60 million of the total U.S. population estimated by the Census Bureau.[2] Of those, over half are estimated to be online in some form and connected to the

Internet. The numbers speak for themselves and highlight that many millions of parents are challenged with the dilemma of how to protect their kids. According to a survey commissioned by Cox Communications and NCMEC, 71 percent of teens age 13 to 17 have reported receiving messages online from strangers; 45 percent have been asked for personal data by someone they don't know; 30 percent have contemplated a one-on-one meeting with an online acquaintance; and 14 percent have actually had a face-to-face meeting with someone that they've conversed with over the Internet.[3] Another alarming statistic is that 40 percent of teens say that they'll respond to a blind or unknown chat request.[4] Research also suggests that 61 percent of teens age 13 through 17 have a personal profile or Web page on a social networking site such as Friendster, MySpace, or Xanga.[5] Of those, approximately 50 percent have also posted pictures of themselves online for view by the full public or their online friends.[6]

Teachers, school administrators, lawmakers, and law enforcement professionals are *not* entirely responsible for protecting today's children. They can help and clearly play an integral part. That said, it's the *parents'* responsibility to educate children about the risks of going online, make the right call as to when they should be granted access to these technologies, and take responsibility for properly raising their children. Parents and teachers today have to get smart on technology and use it to their advantage. No more excuses.

THE INTERNET: WHAT IS IT?

The Internet, simply put, is a collection of millions of computers around the world that are interconnected via wires, wireless, and sometimes satellite connections using computer protocols, networking devices, security appliances, and Internet providers enabling businesses and individuals to access and share information. Although many have contributed to the success and sometimes scary elements about the Internet today, it is appropriate to highlight some of the key milestones and individuals that contributed to this communications medium that may be relative when explaining strategies for protecting children (see Figure 1.1).

On February 7, 1958, the U.S. Department of Defense (DOD) established the Advanced Research Projects Agency (ARPA), which was intended to provide "for the direction or performance of such advanced projects in the field of research and development as the Secretary of Defense shall, from time to time, designate by individual project or by category."[7] It was essentially a response to the Soviet Union's launch of the first artificial satellite, *Sputnik*. Over the years, ARPA's name flip-flopped between ARPA to DARPA (Defense Advanced Re-

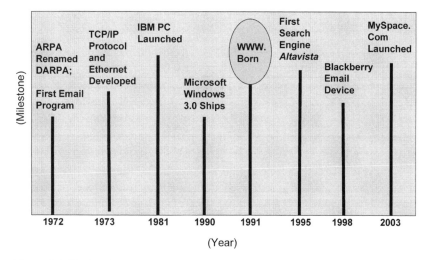

Figure 1.1 Modern Internet-Related Technology Timeline

search Projects Agency) until settling with the final name of DARPA in 1996 as a result of Public Law 104–106, under Title IX of the Fiscal Year 1996 Defense Authorization Act.[8]

In 1962, J. C. R. Licklider of the Massachusetts Institute of Technology (MIT) penned a series of memos outlining his galactic network concept, where he described a series of interconnect computers.[9] In 1962, another MIT researcher, Lawrence G. Roberts, went to DARPA to develop the ARPANET computer network.[10] In 1969 and with the assistance from the group Bolt Beranek and Newman (BBN), the first node of the network came into play at the University of California at Los Angeles (UCLA).[11] By the end of 1969, four host computers were connected into the initial ARPANET—UCLA, SRI at Stanford University, the University of California at Santa Barbara, and the University of Utah.[12] In short, ARPANET became the Internet and as a result, DARPA is essentially the inventor of the Internet as we know it today. Folks from DARPA back in 1958 and even through the late 1960s could not have imagined the types of technologies that we see today that would stand on the incredible achievement of building an information superhighway.

Another great invention was electronic mail, or email. In 1972, Ray Tomlinson at BBN wrote the "first initial hot application"—electronic mail, or email as it is commonly referred to today.[13] While working with other researchers at DARPA, Tomlinson made history when he created the email name format, including the @ sign.[14] According to the Internet Society, "he sent himself a message, the contents of which have been lost in time."[15] Over 25 years later, the first email program, written by Steve Dorner at the University of Illinois, was made available to the public.[16] It was called Eudora, and it changed the way human beings communicate around the globe.

Vinton Cerf, hailed by many as the father of the Internet, invented the TCP/IP protocol, which allows computers of different operating systems (Windows, Apple, Unix, etc.) to communicate.[17] Though not a sexy invention, the TCP/IP protocol is the core of how the Internet works and is installed on almost every computer worldwide, and thus is a major milestone for technology. The IP address is essentially a unique address for a device that is connected to the Internet. Today, most organizations and computers are running version 4 of the IP protocol, commonly referred to as IPv4. IPv4 is essentially a 35-year-old technology that has a limit of approximately 4.2 million individual IP addresses.[18]

IPv6, developed in the 1990s and starting to be implemented, will allow for literally trillions of IP addresses for the future.[19] Why is this important? Because IPv6 is foreshadowing a future that will include a broad array of consumer and professional devices, including watches, cameras, PDAs, cars, MP3 players, and telephones, that will always be online and connected to the Internet. IPv6 will enable the proliferation of these devices; within years, people will be carrying multiple devices that can access the Internet in real time.

Ray Tomlinson, with BBN, is credited with writing the first email program in 1972. Email is one of the major milestones in technology that has persisted for well over three decades. It is the most used Internet application today, for businesses as well as for consumers. I get over 100 emails on a normal day for business and about 10 or so personal messages. Those who are connected to the net use email more often than they do any other technology, including a telephone. Email is the de facto method of online communication today, followed closely by instant messaging. Hail to Tomlinson for getting us started!

In 1974, the first microprocessor was invented, followed shortly by the first commercially available personal computer from Apple Computer, called the Apple II. in 1977.[20] This was a major milestone in the history of computing and Steve Jobs, Apple's brilliant CEO, was leading the way. This brilliance, however was interrupted in 1981 when IBM introduced the personal computer or PC.[21] IBM's PC and Compaq's clone quickly caught on in the corporate workplace and has become the gold standard for business computing.

In November 1985, the world changed when Microsoft released the Windows 1.0 operating system.[22] Between 1985 and 1992, Microsoft made several upgrades to Windows and hit the big time, convincing businesses with it's 3.1

version.[23] The rest is pretty much history. Microsoft went on to dominate the PC operating system market as well as capture a significant portion of the server-based market that runs today's Web and commerce sites, corporate databases, and even popular email programs. Although Apple Computers is still around today and produces desktop and laptop-based operating systems, its share of the operating system market is well below 10 percent. As a result, Apple has successfully transformed itself into a non-PC consumer product company, focusing on music players like the iPod and download services like iTunes. Without them, Apple would have gone away a long time ago.

In 1991, the World Wide Web (WWW) was launched by CERN, the European organization for Nuclear Research and the world's largest particle physics center that resides on the French–Swiss border near Geneva, Switzerland.[24] Tim Berners-Lee of CERN is credited with the birth of the World Wide Web by creating the hypertext markup language, or HTML, which is used to display content from Web sites in a browser running on a computer.[25] In 2004, Berners-Lee was formally recognized for his accomplishment when he won $1.23 million along with the world's largest technology award—the Millennium Technology Prize—by the Finnish Technology Award Foundation.[26] According to CERN, the first Web server in the United States went into production in December 1991 at the Stanford Linear Accelerator Center in California.[27]

In 1993, the University of Illinois National Center for Supercomputing Applications (NCSA) released the Mosaic browser software in a Windows-based graphical user environment.[28] This technology was one of the most important developments in the history of the Internet because it was responsible for displaying Web pages by translating the HTML coding in documents to an easy-to-read page. The rest of the browser software story can be summed up with two companies—Netscape and Microsoft. According to CERN, in 1993 the NCSA released version one of the Mosaic browser application that allowed users to surf the Internet in a user-friendly and Windows-like environment on computers running the Unix operating system.[29] Versions for other computer systems followed shortly thereafter, and by late 1993, there were approximately 500 known Web servers on the Internet.[30]

Marc Andreessen, the leader of the Illinois team, and Jim Clark, a founder of Silicon Graphics, founded Mosaic Communications in 1994, and it was later renamed Netscape Communications. Their product, the Netscape Navigator Web browser, quickly became a success and was hailed by many as one of the most important software applications written in the modern computing era. By the end of 1994, the Internet had approximately 10,000 servers online, 2,000 of which were for commercial use with approximately 10 million users going online after the information posted.[31] By 1995, Microsoft had entered the browser war competition when it released its Windows 95 operating system with a built-in browser application, Internet Explorer. What ensued over the next five to eight years was a hard-fought browser war that Microsoft went on to dominate mainly by catching up to Netscape on technology capability and the fact that they essentially gave the product away, causing Netscape to do the same, but a little too late.

Another key milestone in the history of the Internet came in 1995 when Digital Equipment Corporation (DEC) introduced the powerful search engine Altavista.[32] DEC was an early adopter of the Internet and one of the first commercial companies to launch a public Web site. Altavista quickly became the de facto Internet search engine for two primary reasons. First, it became popular for the vast information that it seemed to offer as a result of an aggressive spider and search of public Web sites. Second, it was a hit with users because of the amazing speed at which it provided results.

Today, search engines are an interesting challenge for parents and educators when trying to protect children from harm while online. They allow minors to quickly hone in on content that may not be appropriate with just a few words typed into a query box. Google is by far the most popular search engine available today, with quick access to billions of pieces of content, images, and information on the Web in a variety of languages. Its name has become a pop culture icon and is often used as both a noun and a verb. It's quite common to Google (or search) for somebody on the Internet to find out more about them. The founders at Google came up with the name from the term *googol*, which is the mathematical term for the number 1 followed by 100 zeros.[33] Though not the number one search engine today, Altavista still exists, and its technology has been licensed and embedded into many other commercial software products that search extensively within them.

In 1998, Research in Motion (RIM) introduced the Blackberry instant email device about a decade after the company was founded in Waterloo, Ontario, in 1984.[34] This unique device, sometimes referred to as a Crackberry because of its addicting nature, is more commonly called a personal digital assistant (PDA) and is one of the most popular tools used in business and government, with millions of paying subscribers. The Blackberry revolutionized receiving email by packaging nearly instant send and receive capabilities that didn't require users to manually check for new mail. That differs greatly from Webmail packages and sites where users have to periodically check to see if they have new messages. In addition, the folks from RIM (as well as other PDA competitors) have packaged a number of additional capabilities into their products, most important, instant messaging, voice, and Internet browsing. I use a Blackberry as my phone, calendar, instant email, and Web browser and find it to be nearly impossible to do without it as I manage my work and home life. The PDA has thus become a modern success and will also complicate the task of protecting children by moving the access point from the home or school into the palm of the user's hands.

One final invention that deserves recognition is the notion and technical capabilities within today's social networking Web sites. Social networking sites are simply places for people to interact, share information, and communicate online. The most popular sites are MySpace, Xanga, and Facebook. Founded in 2003, MySpace is probably the most popular site with millions of members. These sites typically are good draws for people that want to interact and socialize online with many different types of other people that they may never meet in person. Users can post content, pictures, videos, and favorites lists and build friendships and even romances with others. Many sites also offer online chat forums with hundreds of thousands of forum topics to choose from. Although popular with teens and adults alike, it's amazing to see how much information members of these sites disclose about themselves to potentially millions of other strangers. Therein lies the risk to minors—they are often exposed to controversial topics while logged into these sites, or they expose too much about themselves, putting them at risk, potentially to sexual predators. Social networking is here to stay and seems to be a popular method for socializing in cyberspace.

Today, the Internet is used by so many people it's hard to even gather accurate statistics because thousands of new users get online daily. According to a *Wall Street Journal* article, as of May 2006, 143 million Americans accessed the Internet from home, with 72 percent of them connecting via a high-speed data connection.[35] Statistics compiled from the Computer Industry Almanac, a firm that publishes market research reports for the technology sector, show an unbelievable growth that is simply staggering:

- In 1995, the number of Internet users was 45 million.
- By 2000, that number reached 420 million.
- In 2005, the number of users going online surpassed 1 billion.
- By 2011, the number of Internet users is expected to surpass 2 billion.[36]

Of the current 1 billion plus users of the Internet, the top six countries that make up approximately 50 percentage of the total user base includes the United States (18.3 percent), China (11.1 percent), Japan (8 percent), India (4.7 percent), Germany (4.3 percent), and the United Kingdom (3.3 percent).[37] As one of the leaders in Internet usage, the number of U.S. online users is nearing 200 million, which would account for more than half the total population.[38]

More and more children are using computers, either at home or in school. According to a 2003 study released by the National Center for Educational Statistics (NCES) in the United States, 91 percent of children ages 3 and over in nursery school through grade 12 use computers, and 59 percent of them have access to the Internet.[39] Despite the sheer number and growth of youth using the Internet today, there still appears to be a digital divide between races for access at home versus in school. The NCES study goes on to report that 54 percent of white students use the Internet at home, compared with 26 percent of Hispanics and 27 percent of blacks.[40] Internet use by poverty level flip-flops for children who use the Internet at only one location, with 30 percent of use at home and 60 percent of use at school for those under the poverty line versus 63 percent use at home and 33 percent of use at school above the poverty line.[41]

Regardless of access privileges, the challenges associated with protecting minors is daunting enough given these statistics, but what is really scary is that anticipated growth for online access is based on an accelerating increase in mobile devices, such as smart phones and PDAs, especially as price points drop to bring mobile devices to more socioeconomic groups. That's where things will get tricky in trying to lock those devices down.

So why is all of this important to parents? Because everything that kids will learn as they move through middle and high school and into college is based on past computer history, protocols, and operating systems. Simply put, without understanding the technological building blocks, parents don't have a chance at protecting their kids from the risks of going online.

RECOMMENDATIONS

The Internet is a wonderful resource that offers a plethora of information, knowledge, truths, fallacies, and yes, risks, too. It is the world's electronic stage, where companies conduct business, market and advertise their products and services, and billions of messages get sent to and from one person to another. It's a haven for academics, a place of worship for the religious, the conduit for today's pornographers, and the stealth superhighway for predators and criminals. Most parents are both scared by computer technology and marvel at the advances made in the past couple of decades. Many adults take control of their lives and teach their children to lead a moral and good life, but most don't know how to guide their children to the safe content and away from the harmful information on the Internet. Parents that think they understand the risks and computer technology usually really don't. Most are sold mediocre standalone software packages designed to be only part of the solution to safety on the Internet.

Children between the ages of 8 and 17 are not growing up in an environment similar to their parents' childhoods. Children of past generations couldn't even fathom the kinds of hard-core pornography available today at the click of a mouse, nor predict the actions of today's teens while they are online. Start this journey by taking an inventory of all devices and programs available to you that can connect to the Internet. The following recommendations are designed to help parents gear up for the online world and start parenting with confidence by using technology.

- Spend time getting up to speed on the operating systems that are in use in your home. Read up on user accounts, password management, and privileges so that you'll be ready to create effective user accounts for your children with limited rights that prevent the ability to install software. Read up on the administrator account and privileges. This account or accounts with administrator privileges has the ability to manage the computer's operating system, all accounts, and passwords.
- Take inventory of all computers in your home and write down the user IDs and passwords for each person that have access to the Internet.
- Take an inventory of the computer programs and version numbers used in your home, including email, Web browsers, instant messaging tools, voice-over-Internet systems, anti-virus, anti-spam, and Internet filtering/monitoring software. The more applications and devices with online access, the more complex it is to create a safe computing environment. A simple way to take inventory of the programs running on your Windows-based computers is to click the Start button, then Control Panel, then Add or Remove Programs. Windows will build a list of application programs that are installed on that computer.
- Talk to your kids and ask them questions about what they're doing online. Sit down with them when they go online. If you get resistance, your children might have something to hide.
- Review the Web sites your children are visiting for each computer with online access. This will provide an insight into their online activities, including visits to adult Web sites and social networking sites such as MySpace or Facebook. For Internet Explorer browsers, from the browser's menu, click View, Explorer Bar, then History to see a list of previously viewed Web sites. Pressing Ctrl+H is a shortcut. For other browsers, consult the owner's manual or Help menu.
- Search your home computers for pictures and videos. Look for all *.JPG,

.JPEG,.GIF, *.MPG, *.MPEG (common photo and video file formats). This provides a good glimpse into what's been stored, copied, and possibly left over from an Internet browsing session. Surfing the Internet often leaves behind temporary files, including pictures. The easiest way to do this is to double-click and open the My Computer icon, click on Search, select the pictures, music, or video link, select Pictures and Photos and Videos, then click the Search button.

- Take an inventory of all devices—PDAs, phones, computers, laptops, TVs, and so on—that have access to the Internet.
- Ask your kids how many email accounts they have, if they use instant messaging programs, if they have a profile on a social networking site, and where they use computers outside of your home. Honest answers include school, the library, and other kids homes, which can sometimes be the greatest risks. Be prepared for some lies.

Back to School

Training is everything. The peach was once a bitter almond.

—Mark Twain

INTERNET TECHNOLOGIES DEFINED: EDUCATION 101

I feel for today's parents. Most feel technically challenged, frustrated that their teenagers know more than they do about computers, and don't have any idea where to start to fix things so that they can be aware of what their kids do online and proactively protect them from the risks. A key part of this book is to get parents up to speed with technologies that their kids are using or will be using in the very near future. I'm an educator of over 10 years, and I tend to discuss the building blocks associated with a topic before delving into details, strategies, and recommendations. This chapter defines some key technology terms and describes why parents need to know about them as they build an effective strategy for keeping their children safe. As stated previously, the Internet is composed of millions of interconnected computers (PCs and servers), through myriad wiring and technology devices through Internet providers (see Figure 2.1). All computers have an operating system, computer protocols to connect to the network, and a series of applications (browsers, email, instant messaging, etc.) that facilitate online activity.

Because few people read a glossary and to help you get up to speed with technology terminology, this chapter gives parents and educators the basics of some key topics along with an explanation as to why the technology is important

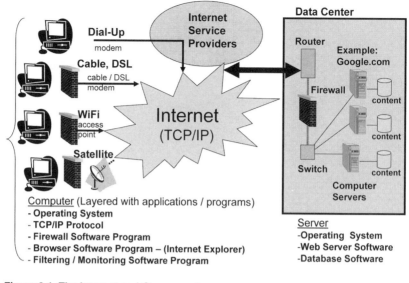

Figure 2.1 The Internet and Components

and relevant in helping to protect children. They are listed in alphabetical order for convenience.

Administrative accounts/privileges: Administrative accounts control what other accounts on that computer can do, such as what directories they have access to or even what programs others can run. Most operating systems have an administrative account. Windows XP does, and it can be used to set up other user accounts and security for a particular computer.

Why it's important: Parents can set up accounts for their children in such a way as to block them from using certain programs that may be harmful or conflict with your work. It's common for parents to set up separate user accounts for each of their children and add the programs that they can see and run. Thus, it's possible to block the Internet for one child and allow it for another by using the administrator account associated with a computer's operating system. Also, most monitoring and filtering software requires administrative rights or has to be installed by the administrator user account. *It is therefore essential that parents know and retain the password for all administrative accounts for computers in their home.* If your kids change their account password on the computer, you'll be able to reset it.

Blocking software: Programs that are installed on computers to block or prevent access to a particular Web site or group of Web sites by information categories (such as adult content). These programs can bet set up to block sites and other Internet-related technologies like instant messaging or voice-related services.

Why it's important: As children get older, it becomes necessary to block access to harmful sites. Parents need to know how to install these types of programs, how to configure their options for blocking sites and categories, and how to interpret usage reports that show what's being attempted but blocked. Teachers in many states will come in contact with such programs as a result of legislation requiring their use in public schools.

Blog/blogging: A kind of diary or online journal on the Internet (a contraction of *Web log*). Many social networking sites like MySpace have features that allow their members to post messages, content, images, and videos online for either semi-private or public viewing. Interestingly enough, more and more teens are using alternatives to MySpace because parents are aware of it and actively blocking it. There are many alternative sites that pose the same risk, and parents need to keep up with them and treat blogging sites as a category and not just by name. Stealth monitoring can come in handy to see exactly what your child is doing online.

Why it's important: Blogging can be fun, yet dangerous. Children have a tendency to post and expose too much information online and put themselves at risk of dangerous solicited and unsolicited content and requests. Sexual predators often look for addresses and other personal data that they can use to approach their victims. Parents need to know if their children use blogs, what they post, and whether they're at risk. Internet monitoring software is an effective way to do this.

Browser: The program that one uses to surf or browse the Internet and Web sites. Browsers are software programs that are installed on top of a computer's operating system that uses underlying computer protocols to communicate to the Internet. Browsers are available for multiple different computer operating systems, including Macintosh, Microsoft, and a variety of Unix versions. Popular browsers include Microsoft's Internet Explorer (IE), Mozilla's Firefox, and Apple's Safari.

Why it's important: Parents need to know how to configure and use features available in today's browsers. These include the use of cookies, seeing the history of sites viewed, blocking sites, and setting security and content levels to protect children. Simply put, a downloaded version from the vendor without any configuration settings may be a security risk to your computer as well as the user and your child.

Cable/Cable Modem, DSL/DSL Modem: A device that connects a single computer or multiple computers to the Internet. It's essentially your direct connection to an Internet Service Provider (ISP), whose job is to connect your computers to a corridor on the Internet.

Why it's important: Parents don't need to know the ins and outs of cable or DSL modems, just that they are the device that connects a computer to the Internet. As technology has evolved, wireless devices are becoming more common. Thus, computers today can potentially gain access to the Internet via another person's cable or DSL device if they have a wireless device connected to it. So why is this important? If the speed on your Internet connection is slowing down and you have a wireless device or access point connected to your DSL or cable modem, someone may be hijacking your Internet connection. If the information that is being sent and received on that connection is not secured via encryption technology, your personal information may be compromised.

Cache: Space on a hard drive where files are stored during normal use. Caches, which can be permanent or temporary, are used to speed up data transfers and certain types of activities, such as browsing the Web. Examples of caches include temporary directories and files when using word processing or spreadsheet programs. Software makers typically design an auto-backup feature that keeps a copy of the file you working on to protect it from being inadvertently deleted.

Why it's important: Most browsers have settings by default that store Web pages previously viewed on the hard drive in a cache. Kids that want to hide their online activities will typically delete the cache with the click of a mouse in the configuration settings of their Web browser. For those that don't delete cache manually, the browser manages the cache as it sees fit and deletes old content as the files grow too large. If not deleted, you can check a fair portion of the files or Web pages your children have previously viewed simply by browsing to the cache directory and opening the files in a browser. It's just one way to get a glimpse of what your child is doing online. If the cache on your home computer is always empty or deleted, your child may be trying to hid something.

Chat/chat room: A place where a computer user can go to converse online with other users. Chatting is a common online and real-time Internet activity.

Not all chat rooms are harmful, but beware—there are a lot of adult and sexual chat sites out there ranging from ones that talk about graphic sex (heterosexual and homosexual), sadomasochism, bondage, and even bestiality. Users must typically enter or log in to a chat room to begin conversing with others online. There are hundreds of thousands of chat rooms hosted and sometimes monitored by a variety of Internet service companies.

Why it's important: Parents must understand the risks of letting a child have access to chat rooms or entering one. Most children use an alias name when entering a chat room to hide their true identity. Online predators do the same, often posing as other teens in attempt to start up a conversation that may lead to a youth exposing personal information that can potentially lead to an in-person meeting.

Cookie: A cookie is a small file that is placed onto a computer by a Web site after visiting the site. A cookie can store information about the visitor, such as name, account number, last visit, user preferences, online purchasing information, or even a password to the site. Many banks and professional Web sites use them to recognize their customers with a friendly "welcome back, Greg" message when they reenter the site. Browsers can also be configured to notify a user when a cookie is about to be downloaded and placed on the hard disk. Those that use this feature can simply accept or reject the pending cookie.

Why it's important: Cookies can be used to track where a user goes online. Many children accept cookies for their email systems so that they don't have to keep entering a password when they go online to check email. That said, cookies are essentially a useful tactic for Web site developers but a mild invasion of privacy. Kids who want to keep their Web sites hidden from parents will often delete cookies stored on their computer after they're done browsing. They do this by simply clicking a button in the browser's configuration menu. Parents who want to see where their kids are going online can view the cookies directory for their particular browser. Consult the documentation for the browser of choice or simply search for "help cookies" and more information will be displayed.

Cybersex: Sexual discussions or online conversations pertaining to the topic of sex or sexual acts. Some adult sites allow for these types of online chats and integrate real-time video feeds that can show graphic sexual situations and acts.

Why it's important: Parents need to be aware that there are some very adult and graphic sites on the Internet that go beyond just viewing nude photos or sexual situations. A good Internet content filtering program will likely block access to most of these sites, but the software companies simply can't keep up with the number of them and how some of them are disguised via innocent names. Cybersex can also occur via the use of other common technology programs, such as email or instant messaging. To get up to speed on what's out there, simply type in one of the following search keywords and be prepared to view some hard-core material: xxx, porn, cybersex, *or sex. Parents must employ a combination of Web content filtering technology, parental policies and rules, and if necessary stealth software to reveal exactly what your child is doing online.*

Data key: A small, portable device capable of storing large amounts of files and content; also called a flash drive or a thumb drive. Most data keys connect to computers via a USB port, usually located on the front or rear of a computer. Newer and larger devices, some as large as several gigabytes, can store thousands of files. These devices are essentially mini-hard drives that are capable of storing files permanently after a computer is turned off.

Why it's important: Data keys or flash drives are small and portable, making them ideal choices for teens who want to store and potentially hide content from his or her parents. If a file retrieved from email or downloaded from the Internet is only stored on a data key and not the local hard drive on the actual computer, it becomes almost invisible to the parent monitoring their computer. Thus, pay attention to what devices are connected to your home computers when your children are online and if necessary, employ monitoring applications that can show all of their activities, including storing or copying content to small portable devices. If your child has such a portable drive, ask to see it from time to time. Review the content on it, and don't take no for an answer. If a child is unlikely to turn over a thumb drive, they might have something to hide. If you think that kids today aren't creative and will always turn over controversial or objectionable content to their parents—you are dead wrong. Even good kids have things to hide and are curious. Flashback—the thought *never* crossed my mind to give the *Playboy* magazine that my friend gave me for my birthday to my parents. I was curious and made an active attempt to hide it. Your kids are likely the same—good kids, curious, and protective of their stuff as they get older.

Domain name: A domain name identifies the name of the computer (PC or server) where a particular Web page or document is stored. Behind every domain name is a unique address called an IP address that identifies the exact computer. In the example of www.yahoo.com, yahoo.com is the domain name. The domain suffix, .com in this case, identifies the country, organization, or enterprise; .com is for business, .edu is for education, .org is for nonprofit, .mil is for U.S. military, .gov is for U.S. government, and so on.

Why it's important: The domain name tells you where your child has been on the Internet. Most computer logs and monitoring software will list the locations and sites by domain name that your child has visited. Beware—not all domain names are as friendly as they appear. A simple name could easily be hosting and displaying inappropriate content to your child so you may need to go beyond just the name to find out what's behind the web front door of their site. For example, *www.whitehouse.com* which has adult content, versus *www.whitehouse.gov* which is the actual White House.

Email: Email is the most common form of online communication today. Almost anyone that goes online has one or more email accounts. Some are free, and others are paid, such as ones with your name in the domain (Example: person1@gregoryssmith.com). There are a variety of email programs on the market; some are preinstalled on a computer, and others are Web-based and thus only require a browser to access.

Why it's important: Web-based email accounts are more common for teens than ones that are installed on an actual computer. Why? Because a child with access to the Internet can sign up for one, potentially without their parents knowing about it. Risks of email for minors include unsolicited messages from businesses and other strangers, some with legitimate content, others with sexually explicit messages, pictures, or links to pornographic sites. Chapter 7 goes into much more detail on this topic, including when to allow your child to have an email account and how to monitor it to minimize risk.

Encryption: Encryption is typically a software program or algorithm that scrambles messages, content, Web sites, and so on from one computer to another. Essentially, it makes the online communication nearly impossible to intercept, read, or monitor. The U.S. government maintains encryption keys to unlock and view secure sessions, but parents do not have access to this to find out what their kids are doing.

Why it's important: More sites, including adult hard-core pornography, and IM tools are using encryption to prevent programs and firewalls from blocking their traffic to your home computer. Most home and business computers allow encrypted sessions to flow to the Internet, usually through port 443 on a firewall. All online banking, stock trading, and financial sites use them to secure transactions. By encrypting a pornographic Web site or IM session, the Web site owners are trying to make it more difficult to block access to their sites. Chapters 5 and 6 goes into strategies to detect and block pornographic content, regardless of whether the site is encrypted. Stealth monitoring is often very effective to reveal exactly what your teens are doing online—regardless of whether the session is encrypted.

File sharing programs: A file sharing program is a software application that facilitates the distribution of content, usually photos, videos, and music, from one computer to another. These programs usually require software to be installed before one can share or download from another computer. The most common examples of file sharing sites include Napster, Kazaa, and Limewire.

Why it's important: Many of these programs facilitate sharing of illegal files or content. A recent example includes the evolution of Napster from a free service that facilitated the illegal transfer of music files to a fee-based service that is now legitimate. Other risks of these types of programs include the capability for other users on the Internet to be able to browse limited directories on your computer, potentially exposing personal data. Thus, proceed with caution with regard to file sharing programs. They can open up your computer to outside eyes.

File transfer protocol (FTP): A protocol for downloading and uploading files. FTP sites are simple servers that facilitate downloading and sharing of content. Most companies have FTP sites so that their customers can download updated programs or bug fixes for software they make and sell. FTP sites are essentially a poor man's file sharing site. Some are secure, and others are completely wide open to the public. An example of an FTP site is designated by ftp://username@ftp.company.com , where the username may or may not require a password.

Why it's important: Some teens that share files on FTP sites can create an FTP server on your home computer if they have administrative rights to do so. Thus, they can download content from others or turn your home computer into an Internet showroom without your knowledge, potentially exposing personal content about themselves or your family. In addition, there are a variety of FTP sites that offer hard-core pornography with somewhat cryptic names, making them difficult for parents to detect. Not all FTP sites are blocked by filtering software and can therefore introduce content risk to teens. FTP sites are alternatives to getting content from standard Web sites. Blocking FTP as a service is an option at the firewall, but then no FTP sites can be accessed. These sites need to be managed and monitored just like standard Web sites. Chapters 5 and 6 talk about how to monitor and block FTP sites if necessary.

Filtering software: Filtering software is used to prevent access to a particular Web site or type of content. Many filtering programs are configurable and allow parents to permit and deny content by categories, such as adult, sports, shopping, and so on. Filtering programs come in two flavors—ones that are installed on your computer or ones offered as a service via your Internet service provider. If configured properly, they can be somewhat effective, but not foolproof.

Why it's important: This software is popular with many parents today, and there are a variety of providers on the market. Filtering software, however, will not fully protect your child. More Web vendors are devising schemes to bypass filtering software algorithms. Most popular search engines offer a backdoor glimpse into adult porn sites by providing thumbnail image results to simple Web searches—even with some of the most sophisticated content filtering products. The links to the sites returned may be blocked, but the images can reveal hard-core sex even with safe searching options turned on. Also, most products can't protect against backdoor threats like friends sharing picture or video files through email or sharing files via data keys. Chapters 5 and 6 go into more detail on this topic and provides parents with more tools to detect and reduce threats. These include recommendations for restricted access for teens to standard search engines like Google and Ask.

Firewall: A firewall can be a physical device or a software program. Its main purpose is pretty simple—to prevent harmful viruses and unwanted content from going into or out of your computer. That said, most firewalls are complex to set up and maintain and require a bit more computer knowledge than what it takes to just browse the Web. Many businesses maintain sophisticated, powerful firewall devices to protect their business information. Home computers are usually protected by one or more software firewalls. Some are built into the operating system, like the firewall by Microsoft, whereas others are downloaded and installed. I believe in the common saying in life, "you get what you pay for." The free Microsoft product built into the Windows operating system is adequate at best. A version worth a look is BlackICE (www.blackice.iss.net). I use a combination of products from Microsoft and F-Secure and configure them to block everything (inbound and outbound) except what I want to flow to the Internet. In conclusion, a firewall when combined with anti-virus software is the gate-keeper of information flowing in and out of your computer to the Internet—and thus pretty important.

Why it's important: By the time most kids reach the teen years, they already know about firewall technology, what it blocks and allows, and how to reconfigure them to pass the type of traffic that they want to see. Thus—parents need to get up to speed on firewalls and lock them down to prevent their children from changing the settings. Firewalls if configured properly can block traffic to file sharing sites, block individual web sites, and block access to FTP sites if needed. Firewalls, used in conjunction with monitoring software, filtering software, and sound parental policies can make for a safe Internet experience in your home. Firewalls also protect your home computer from other potential threats including viruses and spyware by only allowing the ports or services that you want to go in and out of your computer connected to the Internet.

Gamer: This is a person who plays games on the Internet. Many young children play online or computer games as a mechanism to learn techniques, spelling, mathematics, and grammar. Some teenagers become obsessed with Internet games, many of which have online real-time chat capabilities and chat rooms where they share secrets about their favorite games

Why it's important: Gaming can become an addiction and affect children in a negative way, including becoming reclusive and less social. In addition, Internet predators use gaming sites to meet their prey, first building relationships with them and then gathering personal information. Internet games today are not entirely innocent.

Hacker: This is a person that intends to infect your computer with a virus or program that can compromise or steal information and files from you.

Why it's important: Without firewall technology, anti-virus, anti-spyware, and filtering software, your computer may be at risk. Kids today have an uncanny way of exposing risk to your computer just from the Web sites that they visit. Many gaming sites install software on home computers and create back doors for information, such as online banking passwords, to be collected by an external hacker. Parents need to reign in their kids to protect them from harm on the Internet as well as protect the assets stored on your computers.

Home Page: The top-level page of a Web site. All subordinate pages flow from or are linked to from the home page for a particular site.

Why it's important: Most kids today have one or more personal Web sites or home pages on a social networking site, such as MySpace. Children often expose too much information about themselves that can potentially introduce risk from online predators. In some cases, online Web page postings by minors provide a view into what's on their mind or what they may do in the future. Parents today must be knowledgeable of both the number of Web sites their kids have and the content within them. Monitoring tools (discussed in Chapter 5) provide a road map and set of recommendations.

Hyperlink: A Web page link to another page, site, or document posted on a computer.

Why it's important: Most teens have one or more personal Web sites, and the text alone doesn't always reveal what is on their site. A link to another page or document may be named something straight forward like *homework*, but may actually be a link to other types of content, such as pictures or videos. Most kids don't fully understand the risk of going online or posting too much content about themselves. It's not out of the ordinary for them to disguise content via parent-approved types of content links. Click on them to find out what they expose.

Hypertext Markup Language (HTML): HTML is the language that was invented by Tim Berners-Lee that renders content into displayable pages on the Web.

Why it's important: By the time kids reach age 12 or so, they are well versed at creating Web pages either via a tool or by coding them manually. Some of the tags, usually metatags, in their sites can advertise the site to a number of search engines. Parents may need to learn how to view the source code for their kids' Web pages to see whom they're trying to attract online. This is typically done in a browser by selecting Show source code from the appropriate browser menu on the page that you want to see. Look for words after the tag <meta name="KEYWORDS"> section, which are what search engines use to build their databases.

Hypertext Transfer Protocol (HTTP) and (HTTPS): These are the basic protocols that allow for a Web browser on a computer to communicate with a Web server on the Internet. The *S* at the end of HTTP indicates a secure site.

Why it's important: Sites that use HTTP are not secure. Sites that use HTTPS are encrypted and are typically secured. Examples include online banking sites. However, more porn sites are using HTTPS to bypass firewall rules attempting to block their traffic. Parents should regularly review the list of sites that their kids visit, especially ones that are encrypted.

Instant Messaging (IM): Instant messaging is the newest craze in online communication. Teens to adults are IMing each other to communicate. Most IM tools and services are free. Popular ones include Yahoo! Messenger, MSN, and AOL Instant Messenger. Unlike email, IM tools show when another user is online.

Why it's important: Instant messaging is a common tool used by sexual predators on the Internet. Much of the traffic sent is only logged by the Internet provider, and it also may allow for files to be sent from one computer to another without a proper parental audit trail or log. Many IM programs also encrypt data during transmission to bypass tools designed to block the service and pass through most firewall technology. Last but not least, many IM tools allow users to send and receive voice calls over the Internet. Although this is a great and cool technology, parents have no log of the calls, originators, or content; simply put, your kids might be talking to a stranger or sexual predator. IM use is soaring, and traffic is projected to surpass email traffic by 2010 or 2012, making this technology a real challenge for parents to monitor. Chapter 8 goes into more details about IM and provides parents with solid recommendations on how to monitor and control the risk.

IP Address: An IP address is the unique address of a computer, usually tied to the network interface card (NIC) that is commonly installed or shipped with most computers or devices today. Without getting too technical, the IP address is like the Social Security number of a computer or Internet-enabled device running the TCP/IP protocol that is designed to connect to either an internal data network or the Internet via a cable or wirelessly. An IP address is made up of four sets of numbers separated by periods, and the address can either be private (one that is not registered and exposed to the public) or public. An example of an IP address is 24.120.220.165. Internet service providers give home users access to the Internet by providing them with a fixed IP, sometimes referred to as a static IP address, or a dynamically allocated one at the time that a computer connects. Most dial-up connections to the Internet use dynamic IP addresses because they can be reused by the ISP when the user is no longer online. However, most home users (especially in developed countries) are connecting to the Internet more often with digital (non-dial-up) connections that can be allocated for longer periods of time. Thus, the IP address for a home computer in the United States may very well be always on and static.

Why it's important: Parents don't need to know whether their computers contain public or private IP addresses, but they do need to understand the concept that each device or computer that connects to the Internet will likely have a separate IP address and go through some conduit or channel to get connected to the Net. Teens with wireless network cards enabled on their laptops pose an interesting challenge for parents because they may be able to access the Internet through another connection outside of the home. In addition, the adoption of always-on PDA devices will also complicate putting in parental controls. My BlackBerry is able to bypass strong content filters enabled at work or home, and usage reports by user are not reviewed due to labor shortages. (More on this risk in later chapters with some tips to help mitigate the risks.) To quickly obtain the TCP/IP configuration from a Windows-based computer, open a command prompt (via Start, Run, Command), and type "ipconfig" and press Enter. The results will include the IP address of the network interface (wired or wireless—some computers can have both) along with other technical information suitable for IT pros. The ping command is also helpful to identify the IP address of another computer or Web site. Simply type "ping" followed by the full IP address or Web site (example: ping www.microsoft.com) and press Enter. The results will show the time, usually in milliseconds, that it takes to talk to the other computer (or yours if you ping yourself). As parents get more comfortable with networking concepts, the ping command comes in handy to identify and test connections to wireless access points, firewalls, and other computers in the home that are networked. By the time your kids are in their mid-teens they will have these concepts nailed down, and it will be even more important to keep up with them without calling the Geek Squad.

Internet: As stated previously, the Internet is a collection of millions of computers that are interconnected via wires, wireless, and sometimes satellite connections using computer protocols, networking devices, security appliances, and Internet providers enabling businesses and individuals to access and share information. Information on the Internet consists of useful research, educational materials, corporate sales and marketing collateral, information on products and services, software, and, yes, objectionable content and hard-core adult and child pornography.

Why it's important: Parents have an obligation and right to help protect their children and other minors from dangers that lurk on the Net. In addition, parents and educators alike need to better understand the components and devices that connect to the Internet; the risks; and tools to monitor, block, and filter inappropriate content to properly execute on a strategy to ensure safe computing for minors. More teens are becoming Internet savvy, and parents need to catch up and take a proactive role in granting permission and access to the Internet via the variety of devices and connections on the market today.

Internet Service Provider (ISP): An ISP is the link or conduit to the Internet for a particular computer or device. Examples include (but are not limited to) (1) T-Mobile for BlackBerry PDA wireless email and Internet access, (2) AOL for computer-based access to the Internet and email, (3) Vonage and Skype for phone service over the Internet, (4) Earthlink for home and small business computer access, (5) AT&T for voice, text messaging, and PDA Internet access, and (6) Qwest for business-grade access and high-speed connections to the Internet for larger organizations and businesses. Each ISP maintains the hardware (and sometimes software) needed for their users to connect to the Internet, and most charge a fee to connect, usually monthly. Lower speed connections like dial-up are usually more cost-effective but result in longer times to download or view content. Higher speed digital connections provide a more enjoyable surfing environment that usually results in fast download speeds and quick access to content. ISPs can also supply other services beyond just connecting to the Internet, such as email or Web hosting.

Why it's important: Parents will likely be paying the bill for all of the methods and channels that their home computers and children can access the Internet. It's easy to see how costs can quickly get out of control and increase as most households in the United States have broadband (high-speed) Internet connections for their home computers, as well as multiple cell phone and PDA-enabled accounts that provide access to the Internet. The good news is that you'll know how you're household is connected by the bill you pay, unless of course your child is hijacking a neighbor's unsecured wireless Internet connection without your knowledge or approval.

Java: Java is a software development language invented by Sun Microsystems designed to run on a variety of computer, devices, and operating systems. In contrast, applications typically written for the typical PC running Microsoft Windows requires a specific version of the Windows operating system or Internet browser to run properly.

Why it's important: Java applications are here to stay, and more software developers are writing in Java to allow their applications to run on any computing platform, including the Macintosh, Windows PC, Unix, PDA, cell phone operating system platforms, and more. The BlackBerry device includes a Java runtime client application that enables running Java applications on the PDA itself. Java applications can run on a computer, as a plug-in download file to an Internet browser, or simply as preinstalled software on any device. Most browsers allow administrators to set security protection and either allow or prevent the use of Java applications. Why? Because Java applications can have access to the files and information on a computer and potentially communicate sensitive information to hackers if the application is written to do so. What can parents do about this? Not much, because they generally don't know which applications may be harmful or not. What is important, however, is to only install or run Java applications from reputable firms. Avoid downloading (via blocking the capability to install an application at the account level of your child), any application, Java or otherwise, from online gaming sites, which are frequently used to deposit spyware or programs designed to compromise personal information stored on computers.

JavaScript: JavaScript is a software scripting language used by software programmers to build logic and features into Web-based application pages. Unlike Java, it doesn't pose the same threat of access to information stored on a local computer. Common uses of JavaScript in Web pages include validating data entered into a form—such as an email address, ZIP code, state, or country. JavaScript runs on local computers after the files are downloaded from the Web site being accessed. Most browsers have the capability to turn off JavaScript, but most users allow it.

Why it's important: This technology is really about Web site and application performance than security. The slower the Internet connection, the slower the response to displaying pages with JavaScript embedded in them and the longer it takes to process or submit online forms. A high-speed Internet connection allows JavaScript run much faster. No real harm here.

Monitoring Software: Monitoring software is an application program that is either installed on your computers or used as a service via your ISP to help you potentially block sites, content, and services. Monitoring software can log online activities that include downloading files, accessing Web sites or FTP servers for restricted content, using IM programs, making voice calls over the Internet, and standard email usage.

Why it's important: These programs are not only helpful in protecting children but essential for parents and educators today. Monitoring programs can also be installed in what's called stealth mode so that kids don't even know they are there. Savvy teens will look for monitoring programs running on their computers and may attempt to uninstall them (if they have the privilege on their account) or remove them from memory. A common tactic on computers running the Windows operating system is to press the Ctrl-Alt-Delete key combination to reveal a screen (the task manager) that allows them to see what programs and processes are running. Programs are clearly displayed in the window, and users can easily shut them down if desired. Examples of common programs include a browser, Microsoft Word, and Excel. Many other software applications and monitoring tools are displayed as more cryptic processes. A program is usually made up of one or more processes running in the memory of your computer. Examples of processes that are not displayed as programs include anti-virus and anti-spyware applications. Some processes are easily discernible by their name and can be killed to terminate the application. Other processes are not so obvious and can be difficult for teens to crack and disable. Well-designed stealth monitoring programs fall into this category.

Multimedia (audio, video, etc.): Multimedia files typically display more than just text. Examples include pictures, audio files, and videos. Many of these files are readily available for download and viewing, and some of them come with significant risks. You wouldn't want your teen downloading or viewing a portion of the Paris Hilton sex video clip online. Without proper filters or blocks, files like these are just a click away, usually through an industrial-strength search engine like Google, MSN, Yahoo!, or Ask. Multimedia files come in a variety of types that include common file extensions like .wav, .au, and .mp3 for audio files; .jpeg, .jpg, .bmp, or .gif for photos and images; and .mpg, .mpeg, .avi, .mov, and .qt for videos.

Why it's important: There are many options for formatting content, and several free options including browser plug-ins for viewing or playing multimedia files. Parents need to be cognizant of the types of files and applications that their children use to ensure that they're not at risk. Most pornography is distributed or viewed by images or links to photos from Web sites and email messages. If done properly, images can be embedded directly into the content of an email so that they display on opening without any other action from the user. Users on social networking sites like MySpace frequently post audio, video, and photos that many parents might object to. Although many of these sites have terms of use and methods for reporting questionable content, they don't get all of the bad stuff. And for a lot of them, you don't even have to be logged on or registered to search and find objectionable content.

Access to multimedia content, including adult and hard-core pornography images and videos, is just a click away with the help of a search engine. Parents need to be aware of the file types and content that they provide as well as the most common methods for accessing it. Once you are fully educated, lock down those computers and monitor your kids to see what they're up to. Don't forget those data keys . . .

Operating System (OS): At a high level, an operating system is the key program that controls the basic functions of a computer, which include how software programs get loaded into memory and run, how files get saved onto disk drives, and how data is displayed on a monitor. They come in a variety of version and flavors. Microsoft currently dominates the PC operating system market for home and business computers and laptops. Older versions of their operating system that are still in use today include Windows 98, Windows NT,

Windows 2000, Windows XP, and Windows 2003. Newer versions have become much more proficient and intelligent at performing tasks quickly, adding to the enjoyment of user computing. Other operating systems that are less common in homes and the office include Apple's Macintosh OS and various versions of Linux and Unix. Most popular Web browsers have been adapted to run on all of these operating systems. Because the market share is so large for Windows-based PCs in homes today, this text focuses predominantly on computers equipped and running Windows.

Why it's important: The most important aspect of an operating system for parents to know is how to create user accounts and manage their security. I'm a strong advocate that children should not have user accounts on home computers that let them administer the PC, create new user accounts, change their profiles to allow for more functions like installing software applications and changing passwords. Parents must get up to speed on how to create user accounts for their children that grant them appropriate privileges on their computers. Part of this important role includes password management for all administrative user accounts, Web content and filtering software, and email accounts. Take charge of the computing environment in your family and manage it proactively. One of my colleagues asked me why I thought it was ok to run such a tight ship in my house with regards to computer access to the Internet and whether I thought that it was an invasion of my children's privacy. My answer was swift—*It is my role, right, and obligation to do what is necessary to keep my kids safe and I don't need anyone's permission to take the appropriate actions. They're my kids!* Get up to speed on the operating systems used in your home and kids' schools and, if possible, consolidate to one or two in the home to ease management and administration.

Phishing: This is a common tactic by hackers and scammers to trick users into giving up personal or confidential information like addresses, bank accounts, and Social Security numbers. The most common form of phishing occurs through email and in most instances contains some official-looking text and a link to a Web page where users are encouraged to confirm or change personal content and information about themselves. Banking scams are most common—unsuspecting users are redirected to a bogus Web site that looks like their bank's Web site but isn't. Most phishing sites have IP addresses in the Web link compared to a properly qualified domain name in the link, like www.-Wachovia.com. Some phishing email links also redirect users to sites that can install spyware or other harmful programs designed to collect personal information from home computers.

Why it's important: Parents should be aware of this for their own protection as well as that of their children and need to pay attention to Web URLs when being asked to confirm or edit any personal or financial information online. Most top-level banks have other methods to thwart phishers that include the use of special passwords or image file uploads to their site so that their customers know they are on a secure and authentic Web site. Parents need to talk with their children about not giving out information while on-line—including address and phone numbers, as teens can be more easily duped than adults. Anti-spyware and anti-spam programs are also helpful in an attempt to reduce phishing. Every email account should have these protections. If they don't, close them down and look for a viable alternative that better protects your kids and your personal information as well.

Plug-in: A plug-in is a special kind of program that installs on your computer and works with your browser to enhance going online and accessing content from Web sites. The most common types of plug-in programs facilitate viewing PDF content and documents, viewing pictures, listening to audio or music files, and viewing video within the browser's window. Plug-ins are a great way to enhance the interactive experience.

Why it's important: Some plug-in files can damage your computer or create back door programs that can compromise personal information to hackers and scammers. Accept only plug-ins from reputable sites that have fully named Web pages (Example: www.adobe.com) and not Web sites using IP addresses as part of their domain name. In addition, you might restrict what teens can install, limiting their ability to install a potentially harmful plug-in without your knowledge and consent. This can be easily done by using user account privileges applied to their accounts. Remember, the operating system rules the computer's activities. A simple request by a teen to install software or a plug-in can be overridden by the security settings at the operating system applied to their account. When applied correctly, this is a good safe surfing tactic.

Podcasts: Podcasts are audio files that are accessible for listening online and downloadable to audio players, usually in MP3 format. Most podcasts are played with the assistance of either a browser plug-in or a separate audio player like Windows Media Player or iTunes.

Why it's important: The majority of podcasts are usually recorded and published for business, educational, or product/promotional purposes. Keep in mind that anyone with the right equipment can create and record a podcast, publish it to a Web page, and promote it relatively easily. Podcasts can contain a variety of inappropriate content and discussion. To complicate matters, audio files are extremely difficult to filter and restrict by content filtering software, mainly because the audio is not transcribed to text that can be filtered. Thus, the wrong type of podcast can easily fly under the radar and into the hands of young teens without parents' knowledge. I recommend that parents search their computers from time to time for a variety of file types that include .mp3 and .wav (audio) and play the content to ensure that it's appropriate for children. Look for these files in all hard drive directories and any mobile data keys.

Pornography: Adult-oriented and sometimes graphic sexual content (images, text, and videos) that can include sex with minors, adults (homosexual and heterosexual), and sex acts with animals.

Why it's important: Pornography sites are some of the most profitable on the Internet today. Many require a credit card or paid subscription to access the majority of their content, but a lot have free sections that are teasers for would-be paying customers. These teaser sections can contain graphic content including (but not limited) to all kinds of sex acts. Some adult sites are more extreme than others and provide discreet access to images, photos, and videos. One that comes to mind is Playboy. While appropriate for adults, it is certainly not appropriate for children. Thus, parents today must employ some kind of Internet filtering or blocking software to prevent their children from seeing mature adult content and hard-core pornography. The most common form of access to this type of material is through a standard search engine. Lock them down for children.

Search Engine: Search engines are one of the greatest software inventions as well as the one of the biggest risks for minors for accessing inappropriate content. There are a variety of great search tools on the Internet today including popular search engines like Google, Ask, Altavista, Yahoo!, and MSN. They regularly patrol the Internet, looking for new content to catalog in their search databases. Some search engines offer more content than others. A recent test search using the same keyword, *sex*, revealed 699 million results (or links to Web pages), and another search engine revealed a mere 90 million for the same search word.

Why it's important: Search engines are the most common and easiest way for teens to look for and find inappropriate content. Teens looking for adult content can simply type a variety of keywords into a search engine, which will quickly return millions of Web page links or images. It's just that easy. Several search engines offer safe or family search settings for their users, and these settings do filter search results and block potentially harmful content. The real problem with these sites is that the setting can easily be changed by minors and requires no additional passwords or parental approvals to do so. Thus, most teens can simply set them to not filter search results when they're online, find what they want, save the good stuff to data keys to hide it, set the safe search settings back on, then clear the browser's cache and history to cover their tracks. There are however, alternatives to protecting children from harmful results served up by search engines that include safe search sites and engines. Chapter 6 goes into depth about which search sites are safe for teens along with recommendations on which sites to grant access to your children and how to prevent some really harmful content with search filters that don't work that well.

Secure Socket Layers (SSL): Secure socket layers or SSL is a fancy technical term for a kind of encryption technology. Essentially, SSL is the software that provides a secure session over the Internet to most public Web sites. Financial institutions like banks and online brokerage companies use SSL to encrypt Web sessions from logging on to their site, moving money, and trading stocks and bonds. Browsers typically indicate that a Web session is secure by the placement of a small lock and key icon somewhere in the browser's window. Placing the mouse pointer over the lock will usually reveal the level of encryption is being used. These layers range from weak encryption (40-bit) to strong encryption (128–256-bit). The stronger the encryption, the more secure the sites are and less likely that the site or session (content exchanged between the requesting PC and Web site) will be compromised. In short, this is fantastic technology that has enabled a tremendous growth of self-service Web sites for financial management.

Why it's important: Some controversial sites use SSL to encrypt entire Web sessions and access to their content. Why? Simply put, their operators are getting smarter and are attempting to prevent Web filtering software applications from blocking them. Most firewalls by default allow encrypted SSL sessions through port 443. Blocking SSL essentially prohibits one's ability to do online banking and trading, accessing secure corporate email systems, buying and selling on eBay, purchasing a good or service online with a credit card, or logging into a legitimate but secure Web site to do research that may be available via a subscription. In addition, more instant messaging applications are going secure via SSL to bypass applications attempting to block them. Parents can't get around this one, but note when kids are accessing secure sites and investigate further if warranted. Secure Web sites are typically denoted with an additional "s" in the http protocol section of the Web address, such as https://securelogin.bankname.com. Monitoring software can also come in handy when trying to find out exactly what content your child is accessing from a secure Web site. More in Chapters 5 and 6.

Services: Services are usually programs that run on sophisticated and high-powered servers. Examples of applications that run as services include a Web site or FTP service. As PCs have become more powerful and desktop operating systems more sophisticated, these capabilities are now available on most home computers. Services usually don't show up as applications when a user opens a Windows task manager to view applications and processes running performance and network activity. Services are more complicated and usually show up as one or more cryptic processes running on a computer, making them harder to detect.

Why it's important: A smart teen can turn your home computer into a publicly accessible Web site in a short period of time. If your child has access to the administrator password on your home computer, he or she can set up a Web server and operate a site without your knowledge over your high-speed Internet connection. The site itself and any content displayed may be accessed from anywhere in the world, drawing traffic to your home computer and potentially exposing your new site to hackers and viruses. Parents are encouraged to consult their operating system's user manuals and look for the types of application services that can be enabled. Look for services that are automatically started on bootup. When in doubt, ask your child or set up stealth monitoring to really find out what's running on your home computer.

Social Networking: Social networking sites are Web sites that offer users a forum to share information about themselves with other private and public friends.

Why it's important: Social networking sites are prime target areas for sexual predators. They gather information such as schools, pictures, email addresses, and friends to piece together the necessary types of personal data to launch an assault. Many children don't understand the risks of social networking sites and put themselves in danger by publishing too much private data about themselves. Parents should beware of this technology.

Spam: Spam is simply unwanted email or messages. It comes in a variety of flavors, but the main categories of annoying spam include (1) unsolicited special offers/sales, (2) racially insensitive material, (3) get-rich-quick schemes, and, my all-time favorite (4) adult content. Most companies have sufficient anti-spam solutions in place to reduce (but not totally eliminate) unwanted email, and those algorithms are usually worth the money that organizations spend on them. Junk email can range from 40 percent of incoming email to as much as 75 percent for large multinational and high-worth companies. Free anti-spam solutions are moderate at best in reducing unwanted and sometimes downright profane email. Good anti-spam solutions not only block most unwanted email but also allow users to create and manage their own "accept" and "blocked" lists of email addresses.

Why it's important: Parents will undoubtedly run into email messages that are not intended for children. Inappropriate messages that I've seen from a variety of consumer email products and services include advertisements to grow hair, increase genital or breast size, last longer in bed, or view the latest hot chick's naked pictures. Simply put, parents today *must* pay attention to spam and take precautions to minimize inappropriate content for their children. More on this in Chapter 7, along with clear recommendations on how to see how effective your anti-spam solutions are.

Spyware: Spyware is an interesting phenomenon and fairly recent technology challenge that has significant risks for today's corporate and home computers. In a nutshell, spyware is a program or a script that if downloaded to your computer is capable of causing harm to your system and potentially compromising personal information stored on your system. Many spyware (or adware) programs can turn systems into zombies by taking control of them and using their computing power with hundreds or thousands of other computers to collectively launch an attack against a public Web site, say, Google. Spyware can also store and run simple hard-to-detect programs that can capture user IDs and passwords for what most think are secure financial Web sites. Many companies invest in programs to combat spyware, but few consumers do so. Most consumers I've talked to think that free anti-spyware downloads will get the job done. Let me be frank—in this case, nothing free is really that good. In short, spyware is a dangerous threat that can be protected against if appropriate steps are taken. Chapter 6 goes into strategies for protecting against spyware.

Why it's important: Anti-spyware solutions usually come as separate software products. Spyware can be delivered to computers in a variety of ways. The most common way a computer gets infected is by visiting a public Web site that has been embedded with programs intended to do harm that are downloaded on visiting the site. Common sites that have spyware programs include gaming sites, gambling sites, and pornography sites. Parents can limit the spyware problem via two simple ways: (1) block harmful sites via Internet filtering software, or (2) install and regularly update anti-spyware. The computer industry is evolving, and most anti-virus vendors will employ anti-spyware solutions as part of their offerings in the near future. Thus, parents need to do their research and pick the right products for the job today as well as tomorrow.

Surfing: Another name for browsing the Internet using a standard Web browser. The most common way for adults and children to navigate the Web is to use a search engine to begin finding content. Content found from surfing the Web can come in a variety of forms, mostly from standard Web sites and pages. However, surfing is usually expanded in its definition to include browsing content from social networking sites like MySpace, viewing videos on YouTube, and entering a chat room for a conversation with others. Thus, surfing the Web is no longer classified as just looking at Web sites and pages.

Why it's important: The Internet is a vast resource of information—some truthful, some false. With so much content and the help of sophisticated and powerful search engines, searching the Internet can be a risky proposition in the hands of children. It's quite common for a child to come across inappropriate content as a result of searching for something else. Case in point: Searching for a female friend's name could easily yield pornographic content, including graphic pictures. Parents need to be proactive and set rules for what sites and search engines children have access to and use capable technology to enforce it. In my professional work, I never set a policy that can't be enforced with technology. I apply this to protecting my children as well and it works.

TCP/IP: TCP/IP stands for Transmission Control Protocol/Internet Protocol. In a nutshell, these are the software and networking protocols that allow computers to talk to one another via local area networks or over the Internet. Most computers come already loaded with a TCP/IP software stack so that they can plug into computer networks and the Internet. There's usually nothing to configure at home unless you're setting up a network (wired or wireless) or using a firewall for your home computers. Either way, each device, computer, cable modem, and firewall device has an IP address so that TCP/IP can talk properly.

Why it's important: The only thing that parents need to know about TCP/IP is that it works and requires a unique IP address for each device, whether it be a Windows-based PC, Macintosh, or a computer loaded with the Linux operating system. They all require IP addresses and run TCP/IP. Parents should maintain an inventory of all computers in their house, know the IP addresses for each one, and use appropriate monitoring software for each computer.

Temporary Internet Files: These are files that are stored on a local computer's hard drive that contain actual content (HTML Web pages, pictures, audio, video, etc.) from sites that have been visited. When a user calls up a Web page, the resulting page and content is actually downloaded to the requesting computer's hard disk, retrieved by the requesting Web browser, and then displayed. Once the browser is closed and the computer is shut off, these files usually stay on the local hard drive for some time unless they are manually deleted by the user. Temporary Internet files usually sit in their own subdirectory and can be opened and viewed like they were from a Web page without being connected to the Internet. Most browsers have settings for how these files are managed. Options include setting up a large temporary disk space for improved speed when accessing sites to deleting them once the browser is shut down. The default is usually to let the browser manage an appropriate amount of space, usually a small percentage of the hard disk size, and delete older temporary files as newer pages and sites are viewed.

Why it's important: Parents can get a feel for what their child is doing online by simply using the My Computer icon to search for the appropriate directory and view files stored there. Double-clicking on an HTML file should open the file and display it in the default browser. The default location for temporary Internet files for a Microsoft XP Windows computer is usually stored in a subdirectory for each user. For my computer, it's stored in the following directory: C:\Documents and Settings\Greg\Local Settings\Temporary Internet Files. My browser is automatically set to store up to 596 megabytes of temporary Internet files. Most browsers also allow users to easily view these files. In Internet Explorer, it's as easy as clicking on the Tools menu, Internet Options, General tab, Settings, then View Files. Parents are encouraged to view these files to see what their child is up to. If the temporary Internet directory is always empty, your child may be proactively deleting content from it in an effort to conceal their tracks online.

Text Messaging: Text messaging, or texting, is very popular with the young crowd and even highly used among adults. Essentially, it involves sending a simple message without graphics or attachments, from one device to another. The most popular form of test messaging with teens is through cell phones that are configured to permit outgoing and incoming text messages. Many carriers charge for these messages, some as much as $0.10 per message, so beware of increased costs on your child's phone bill. There are also text messaging capabilities built into to several Web sites that also allow simple messages to be sent from one person to another.

Why it's important: Parents need to understand the risks of texting, especially for younger children. More advertisements and unsolicited messages are being sent to text-enabled cell phones and are exposing children to information that might not be pertinent for them. In addition, texting doesn't leave a good audit trail for parents to review content. In contrast, parents can often review messages sent from and received by their children's email account and even set up forwarding capabilities to allow them to see all inbound messages. Text messages essentially go undetected by parents, leaving children with and an unmonitored communication capability. Grant this technology carefully and when your kids are ready for the responsibility.

Uniform Resource Locator (URL): A URL is a fancy name for a Web address. Figure 2.2 depicts the components in a standard URL and explains each segment.

Why it's important: URLs are the footprints of sites that your children are visiting. Parents should know the kinds of Web sites and pages their children are accessing, including search engines and social networking sites. Most browsers offer a history feature that lists the most recently visited sites. Parents are encouraged to consult their browser's help section and learn exactly how to view this information. If the history list is empty, your child may be deleting it and trying to hide where they've been online.

http://www.domain/directory/sub-directory/file-name.htm
Example: http://www.gregoryssmith.com/profile.html

http	The **HyperText Transfer Protocol** (http), or standard for communication that governs the transfer of several types of web objects.
www	World wide web portion (web pages / sites) of the Internet. Note: Using FTP in this spot would denote a file transfer protocol associated with the web.
gregoryssmith .com	The **domain name** identifies the computer where the document is stored. The domain suffix identifies the country (as in ca for Canada), organization (org), school (edu), commercial enterprise (com) and so on.
profile.html	The document name (or web page) that is stored as a hypertext markup language (htm or html) document.

Figure 2.2 The Uniform Resource Locator (URL)

Webcam/Videocam: Webcams are usually simple and inexpensive camera add-ons (or built-ins) to a computer that allows for taking either still pictures or real-time video of anything in the camera's view. This technology can be used for business purposes to integrate video links into online presentations into a single session, for personal phone calls with video between two parties over the Internet via VOIP, or for sexual situations that often require fees to view the more interesting stuff on the net.

Why it's important: Parents need to know just how easy it is for teens to either proactively or accidentally find this type of live adult content. A recent search for the phrases *+adult +video +cam*, which instructs the search engine to return results where all three words are matched (implied Boolean AND), returned 6.3 million links to sites. Most adult and sex sites allow users to either text chat or video chat with people on the other side of the online video camera, and it can be very easy to get access. Don't believe me? Try the search phrases above to learn just how easy it is to get very adult content and live interactions that are not appropriate for children. Also, if your home computers have Webcams installed on them, pay attention to how your children are using them. It's easy to set one up and expose oneself to the world via live feeds. This technology needs to be monitored by parents. They also need to ensure that content filters are preventing access to adult video and live sex camera sites.

Web Site: A collection of Web pages that usually contains content in a variety of formats and links to other pages within the same site or a different site. The top-level page of a Web site is typically called the home page.

Why it's important: Not only do parents need to monitor what their kids are looking at online, they also should know if their children are hosting their own Web sites. If so, content should be reviewed to ensure that only appropriate material is posted that does not include too much information about themselves—such as personal phone numbers, home/email addresses, or IM names.

Wireless Access Point: A wireless access point is essentially a small computer networking appliance that performs a couple of functions. First, it directly links to a digital broadband or high-speed Internet connection. Second, it can act as a networking switch and allow for computers to be directly connected to it via a data cable. Third, it works with compatible wireless networking cards installed in desktop and laptop PCs to facilitate a wireless transfer of content from the access point to the requesting computer with a wireless card installed in it. Wireless devices are still evolving and come in many flavors with phrases like 802.11b and 802.11g. Wireless access points can be set up to talk to specific computers in the home and do so using encryption technology in an attempt to protect content and Web sessions. Most laptop computers come already equipped with a wireless network card that is ready to integrate with a number of access points. Wireless access points can be configured to be secure or unsecure, open to anyone within range. Using an unsecured wireless access point from a computer without asking permission is known as hijacking an Internet connection. The most common term for a wireless access point is Wi-Fi, which stands for wireless fidelity. The typical range for a wireless access point to a computer is a few hundred feet. WiMax technology, which is coming soon commercially, will broadcast a signal to a range of miles instead of feet, making it even more attractive to teens wanting to go online.

Why it's important: It's not important for parents to understand the intricacies of the various wireless networking options, devices, and versions. It is important however, for them to understand the risks of kids going online via a wireless connection that might not be controlled in their own house. This dilemma will only get worse as more powerful and free wireless access points cover a larger geographical range. By the time most children reach the age of 15 or so, they are quite adept at (1) finding unsecured access points, (2) configuring a laptop computer to access a wireless access point, and (3) setting up a wireless access point, including enabling encryption. Parents need to join in and catch up on this knowledge fast. This technology is wonderful, but it can provide several avenues for teens to access the Internet under the parental radar. It's not uncommon for a teenager to use someone else's wireless access point to find inappropriate adult content. Today's teenagers are Web-savvy, smart, and sometimes deceitful. It will become increasingly difficult to lock down a computer and protect minors when the avenues through which they can get onto the Internet fall outside of protections that may be set up within their own homes. Parents need to get up to speed with this technology, install it in their own homes with the assistance of an IT professional, and learn how to lock it down securely. My home network is comprised of a wireless access point connected to a cable modem, employs encryption, and only allows certain computers in the home to use it. Thus—I've blocked my neighbors from hijacking my Internet connection or viewing content as it travels wirelessly from my computers to my access point. Parents—wake up to this technology. Understanding this technology is a key component to protecting kids online.

World Wide Web (www, the Web): The World Wide Web is a broad term for the collection of publicly accessible Web sites. There are millions of Web sites on the Internet, with thousands being added each week. Content is exploding on the Internet as more people join the digital and online revolution. The

Web portion of the Internet is one of the most widely used and known, but it is not the only avenue for people to exchange information and content online. Other avenues include email, FTP, bulletin boards, IM, and voice-over-Internet calls.

Why it's important: Parents need to be up on all of the avenues through which their children can get on the Internet. The Web portion of the Internet deals content displayed via browser software and browser plug-ins. Parents should always think of the Web as the "world wild web" due to the variety of interesting and often inappropriate content that children can find online.

Virus: A program or script that can potentially render a computer useless. Viruses come in a variety of shapes and forms. Some are more dangerous than others. Bad viruses can destroy content on the infected computer and also use that computer to spread to other computers. Viruses attack weaknesses in a computer's operating system. Computers running Linux or the Mac OS are not frequently targeted by coders that write viruses. The majority of viruses are designed to attack computers running one of the many versions of Microsoft's operating system—Windows NT, 98, 2000, XP, 2000 Server, 2003 Server, or any of their application programs designed to run on these operating systems.

Why it's important: First and foremost, parents need to get decent anti-virus software for their home computers. An anti-virus program is only as good as its last update, which can sometimes help protect against hundreds of new virus threats. Decent anti-virus programs for purchase include offerings from F-Secure, Norton, and Symantec. For systems connected to the Internet via digital or high-speed lines, the anti-virus programs should be set to update at least daily (if not hourly). So what does a conversation about viruses have to do with protecting kids online? Not much other than to say that many Web sites that offer inappropriate content for free or fee, such as sites promoting computer games, pornography, and gambling, have a higher probability of delivering a virus than more reputable sites. Some of these sites can also install spyware, which can inflict a stealthy kind of pain that may compromise key passwords to work accounts or even online banking and brokerage accounts. Thus, do your part and block access to these sites for children, and you'll benefit in the long run with fewer viruses and spyware.

RECOMMENDATIONS

It's important that parents and educators stay abreast of recent developments in computer technology and the Internet as a whole. Tools, devices, and technologies change frequently. By the time most children reach 14 or 15 years of age, they have completely surpassed their parent's knowledge of computers and the Internet. If left unchecked, these kids may get into some trouble, whether or not they mean to. Parents have an obligation and right to nurture, educate, and protect their children from the risks associated with going online. Those that feel they are violating their children's privacy by keeping ahead of them from a technology and monitoring perspective may actually be contributing to their risk. That said, I leave you with the following recommendations.

- Take control of all administrative computer accounts and passwords for your computers in the home. Without these controls, you're helpless.
- When your kids are younger and in middle school, place your Internet-enabled computers in a common space that is viewable. Don't allow them to have unfettered access to the Internet, especially from their rooms.
- Get up to speed on firewall programs and learn how they work. They can be very useful in protecting your kids from harmful content and programs as well as any personal or confidential data stored on your home computers. Every computer—home, work, or school—should be protected by either a firewall program or a device.
- Take an inventory of the items and services that have access to the Internet, including computers, cell phones, and PDAs. Reduce risky services where appropriate. Simply put, the fewer devices connected to the Internet, the easier it is to manage them. You may even save some money by restricting or consolidating services.
- Research the types of Internet filters and programs that can block harmful content and monitor online activities. Chapters 5 and 6 may be helpful in this research. No computer or device that is used by a child should be without some type of protection or monitoring. As a parent, you are responsible for what your child has access to or is doing online. Take some responsibility—install and configure software to monitor and filter out adult or objectionable content for minors, and review your children's online activities from time to time. Blocking applications don't prevent all of the risks, which is why I recommend monitoring applications as well. Teens blocked from certain Web sites may get creative and get the content that they're looking for from another, less protected or entirely unprotected computer. They also often share content and files via portable data keys (flash drives), which are easy to hide. Pay attention to what's connected to your home computers and ask to see what's on those data keys.
- Get up to speed on content and security filters that are readily available in

the browser software installed and running on your computers. There may be multiple versions, so take an inventory of the number and type of browsers. It's not uncommon for a teen to download Firefox or Netscape and hide it from their parents, who may only be concerned with security on the installed version of Internet Explorer. If possible, reduce the number of browser applications to one and hone your skills on the settings and capabilities for just that browser.

- Using the administrator account for your computers, set up individual accounts for each child. Where appropriate, restrict those accounts from installing new software or applications. This is commonly referred to as either an administrative or power-user privilege that is associated with a user account. If your child's account has either of these privileges, they can download and install software without your knowledge and configure them to their desires. Lock down your home computers and learn about the operating system's capabilities for assigning security settings by account. No child needs to install software without a parent's consent, unless of course there is stealth software installed.

- Ask questions at your child's school to find out how they are helping protect children using computers in class. Don't settle for generic answers. Get names of products used and discuss and learn about strategies at the school. Engage your child's teacher in a conversation on Internet safety. You may be surprised how little they know.

- Most kids need and use a search engine to do research for school projects. Search engines pose one of the greatest risks for exposing children to adult content. Get your kids using safe search engines instead of a standard version. These include (but are not limited to) Ask Jeeves for Kids (www.ajkids.com), Yahooligans (www.yahooligans.com), or family filtering options on commonly used search engines and sites. Where appropriate, help your child perform the search and approve each results page to ensure that they're not being exposed to inappropriate content. I hate to remind you, but it's your job as a parent to get involved and that includes spending time with your child on the computer and enforcing safe surfing. Chapter 6 provides some additional tips and recommendations on using search engines.

- Last, but not least, keep an open dialog with your children about the risks associated with accessing the Internet and be clear on what tools and sites that they can use.

Risks Overview: Are Parents Making the Grade?

The best way to teach morality is to make it a habit with children.

—Aristotle

AN OVERVIEW OF ONLINE RISKS

Let me be really clear at the start of this chapter—all of the privacy advocates that pontificate about how wrong it is for parents to spy on their kids' activities, some online, in an attempt to keep them safe—can just go pound sand. There, I said it. I don't need anyone's permission to look at my kids' email accounts, see where they've gone online, or even log into their social networking site to see what they've posted privately. I have every right as a parent to do what it takes to keep them safe. My house is not a democracy and is a far cry from a dictatorship, but my rules apply as long as I'm footing the bill. The Internet is definitely an interesting place, especially for parents trying to protect their children from adult content, harmful adult predators, and others intending to physically or emotionally harm children. I write this from Brussels, Belgium, where I'm reminded that technology is global and access to the Internet spans the entire world, even in remote places. As I strolled the streets of this city, I notice a number of Internet cafés that offer access to the Net at an hourly rate, some charging for as little as 15 minutes. I stopped inside one to see who was there and what they were doing. To my surprise, most of the patrons of this particular café were teenagers, with an occasional businessman looking frenzied. Anyway, I glanced at what many of the teenagers were doing as I walked through. Most were using email and updating social networking sites, entering what appeared to be additions to long-winded blogs. Two young boys, likely 15 or 16, were toward the back, and as I approached, they minimized the screen. I caught a glimpse before they cleared the screen entirely, and it looked like they were browsing porn sites. That's when it hit me: Creative kids will look for opportunities to gain unfettered access to the Internet. That said, most children in industrialized countries are exposed to the Internet via four primary uses and locations:

1. computers at home,
2. computers in school,
3. computers at other friends' houses, or
4. Internet cafés or shared Wi-Fi sites like coffeehouses.

According to a Pew Internet and American Life Project Teens and Parents Survey, 87 percent of children between the ages of 12 and 17 (approximately 21 million) use the Internet.[1] In addition, 74 percent of teens most often go on the Internet at home, followed by 17 percent at school.[2] The Pew study goes on to report that overall teens use computers to access the Internet 87 percent of the time at home, 78 percent at school, 74 percent at a friend's house, 54 percent at the library, and 9 percent at a community center, youth group, or community church.[3] The highest percentage of growth in use came at libraries, where reported use went from 36 percent in 2000 to 54 percent in 2004.[4] The Pew survey goes onto report that 60 percent of children as young as sixth grade go online, with the numbers steadily increasing as they get older (82 percent for seventh grade, 85 percent for eighth grade, and up to 94 percent for twelfth grade).[5]

There are a variety of risks and potential harms associated with going online for both adults and minors. The following is a list of some of the consequences that can happen to anyone (see Chapter 4 for specific cases).

- Exposure to sexual content, exploitation, and harassment—potentially from sexual predators
- Computer viruses and spyware
- Hacking attempts to steal personal information
- Gambling and addiction
- Illegal purchase or distribution of drugs
- Exposure to extreme violence and mutilation
- Exposure to racially insensitive/hate content

- Fraud and identity theft
- Personal injury and harm

To keep things simple and help parents and teachers develop a solid road map for protecting children, I've categorized the top five risks of going online into the following general categories targeted toward children between the ages of 8 and 17.

1. Viewing graphic pornography and other adult content
2. Computer viruses, worms, and spyware that can compromise personal content
3. Sexual predators looking for victims
4. Adults looking to inflict other harm on children, including kidnapping, rape, murder
5. Content promoting hate crimes, weapons, and harm to others

These risks can be delivered or accessed in a variety of ways, ranging from simply browsing the Internet, blogging, using email, instant messaging, swapping files between computers, using cell phones and PDAs, or conversing with others in online chat rooms (see Figure 3.1).

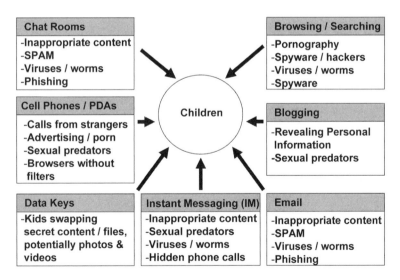

Figure 3.1 Internet Risks Overview

Browsing/Searching

Browsing the Web and using search engines is one of the most common activities for teens and adults online today. Risks of unfettered browsing includes exposure to graphic pornography, risk of spyware being placed on home computers, exposure to viruses, and hackers attempting to steal personal or financial information, such as banking passwords and accounts. I recently performed an experiment and searched for the phrase *sex* on five popular search engines, both with and without content filters. Content filters are essentially efforts by the search site to filter out adult and mature content from being displayed on the results page. Interestingly enough, search engines produce very different results in both the number of search results returned and the effectiveness and security of their family filters (see Table 3.1). Microsoft's new Live.com produced the greatest number of search results, totaling almost 700 million pages, whereas Ask.com produced the least, with just over 90 million page results returned. Three of the five search sites asked for confirmation to turn off family filters and return all results, regardless of content. All of the sites appeared to use cookies to store the search setting (family safe, moderate safe, or no filtering) on the local computer's hard drive. Although the intent by these search firms is good, most teens simply get around the settings by changing them, deleting the cookies, or just downloading another browser and setting their own search settings.

What I found most interesting about these family filters was that they were, for the most part, not effective at all. With the exception of Microsoft's Live .com, all of the other search engines still returned a significant number of results

Table 3.1. Search Results

Search Engine	Returned Links to Pages with Safe Search On (requires cookies to be enabled to work properly)	Returned Links to Pages with Safe Search Off
Google	146 million	599 million (returned 1.5 million graphic images)
Ask.com	90.7 million	90.7 million
Altavista	229 million	393 million (asked to confirm turning off safe surfing)
Live.com	0 (The only search site that worked with strict filters turned on)	695 million (asked to confirm turning off safe surfing)
Yahoo!	236 million	394 million

with family filters turned on. Ask.com didn't seem to work at all and returned the exact same number of links to pages for unfiltered and filters turned on. My point is simple: At 236 million links to pages returned for a site like Yahoo!, it can't possibly be effective at returning family-safe content for children. Even though Microsoft's new tool is a late entry to the search engine family, it impressed me the most and returned zero links to pages when family filters were turned on.

Another risk associated with using a search tools is that they expose children to graphic images. Using Internet Explorer (versions 6 and 7), I set up filters within the browser itself to block harmful content. These work somewhat well, but they are not fully effective. With these settings in place, I attempted to go to a known adult Web site. The content filter setting in the browser appropriately blocked the Web site from displaying content on the screen. I then set the browser to block all sites and only allow those that are approved by a parent (by entering an administrative password) to be viewed. I allowed Google to be one of those approved sites and began searching for adult terms to see what would be viewable. With safe settings on Google turned on and content filters in Internet Explorer set to the most aggressive level, the search tool still returned 146 million links to content pages. When I attempted to view those pages, the browser blocked them as expected. However, when I clicked on the Images tab on the Google results search page, I was able to view images easily, bypassing both filters. When I turned safe searching off, I was able to view graphic photographs with the click of a mouse, bypassing the content filters that had been set in the browser altogether. The nature of the photographs that were easily viewable included close up shots of vaginal, oral, and anal sex.

I recently also ran the image tab test on an expensive, industrial-strength filtering software. The product, Websense, is a software service used by many organizations and is considered to be one of the leading Internet filtering tools on the market. It also failed my test, revealing access to a many graphic adult images that should have been blocked in the first place. These examples demonstrate that software designed to detect and block harmful content may be playing catch-up when compared to sites that want to distribute their information to the masses, regardless of the content rating.

The risks to children don't just stop at being exposed to mature content but also include being a victim of child pornography. According to CNN.com, in October 2006 U.S. federal officials arrested more than 125 people accused of subscribing to a Web site that had content and photographs of children, including infants, engaging in sexual activities with adults.[6] The article states that the suspects included over a dozen convicted sex offenders that had accessed the site starting in late 2005.[7] Disturbingly, among the suspects was a former counselor at a Bible camp, a Boy Scout leader, and middle school sports coach.[8] U.S. Attorney Christopher J. Christie also indicated that such pornographic sites can make up to $2 million per month in subscription fees.[9] These facts clearly support the need for parents and schools to implement separate programs to filter and block harmful content in a way that search engines have not been able to do successfully to date. Security settings within browsers and search engines are not effective enough to protect children from harmful content. The technologies implemented in these tools simply aren't sophisticated enough to determine whether a particular photo, video, or audio is suitable for a child. Most rely on a Web site's ratings (safe, mature, adult) to trigger a content filter. Chapter 5 goes into more detail on how to implement safe browsing environments.

Email

Congressman Mark Foley wrote a series of emails to an underage page working at the U.S. House of Representatives. Foley's online activities, which included lewd and sexually suggestive emails and instant messages, ultimately led to his downfall from politics in 2005.[10] The emails "freaked me out," said a page who was asked by Foley to send a picture of himself.[11] After being warned by Congressman Shimkus, who was responsible for the Page Board, the emails continued and began showing up in newsrooms in Florida.[12] On September 24, 2005, the Stop Sexual Predators Web site published scanned images of Foley's emails sent to pages.[13] By 2006 the event was well publicized in the media and in the fall of 2006, Foley resigned and the FBI launched a probe. According to *Newsweek*, "It is unlikely he [Foley] will be prosecuted unless evidence emerges that he tried to lure minors into physical sex, not just e-mail sex."[14]

Kids give away their email address to too many people and can potentially expose themselves to a flood of unwanted email if they post their address online at social networking sites. The more exposed their email address is, the more potential risk from sexual predators, spam, phishing, and viruses. Many anti-spam filters are simply not effective at blocking inappropriate content from arriving in a teen's email inbox. In addition, some teens send adult and pornographic content as file attachments and disguise the file names as something innocent—easily bypassing content filters. Email and other online tools like instant messaging are common methods that sexual predators use to prey on victims, both adult and underage. Chapter 7 talks about safe email programs, how to protect children from Internet predators, and how to communicate safely online.

Instant Messaging

Instant messaging (IM) tools have become the online program of choice for most children and teens today, surpassing even email as the preferred method for communicating with friends and, yes, strangers. They are easy tools to learn, can be installed on computers and other personal communication devices like PDAs, and, more important, don't usually leave a footprint or audit trail for parents to snoop around and see what their children are doing. Teens like IM because it's a stealth tool of choice. They can go online, converse with friends, meet new ones, and have private conversations beyond their parents' control. In addition, these tools provide technical mechanisms to send file attachments, potentially bypassing anti-virus scans because they can be encrypted. They can even conduct phone conversations over the Internet by simply adding an inexpensive headset to a standard computer.

Unfortunately, IM is also the tool of choice with sexual predators that are looking for teens to chat with and potentially exploit them in hopes of engaging them in sexual activity. A U.S. Justice Department study found that "one in seven children on the Internet has been sexually solicited and one in three has been exposed to sexual material."[15] The article describing this study goes on to list a series of public service announcements supported by the U.S. Attorney General and how they are designed to "warn teen girls against posting images or information that would put them at risk."[16] I support these types of advertisements to raise awareness, but they simply do not do enough to curb risks of going online. Be aware that there are plenty of sexual predators looking to engage in sex acts with young boys (as well as girls). Hundreds have been arrested and prosecuted to date.

To highlight the sometimes open and rude approach that predators take, the following is an excerpt obtained by ABC News from instant messages sent by Congressman Mark Foley, using the screen name Maf54, to an underage male page.

> Maf54: What ya wearing?
> Teen: tshirt and shorts
> Maf54: Love to slip them off of you.
> Maf54: Do I make you a little horney?
> Teen: A little.
> Maf54: Cool.[17]

People like Mr. Foley that are caught or exposed deserve to lose their job at a minimum. These actions, usually calculated and intentional, are not acceptable, and perpetrators should be held accountable and, if appropriate, prosecuted to the fullest extent of the law, both federal and state.

Chat Rooms

Chat rooms are another form of communication favored by teenagers today. They offer a way for people to converse online with others and expose their identity or fly under the radar with a different name or alias. As indicated in a previous chapter, chat rooms are all over the Internet, are offered by a variety of providers, and are easy to use. Most looking for a site simply navigate the various chat room names after searching for one or navigating by chat room title. Once online, users can converse with one another in a real-time conversation—most of which is never logged by the user, but usually by the chat room hosting provider. For obvious reasons, chat rooms, along with IM and email (for one-on-one communication) are the preferred tools by criminals, pornography distributors, and sexual predators. Allowed use and monitoring of these sites are recommended to parents.

Online Predators

So what is an online predator anyway? The typical Internet predator is male, middle-aged, and married with children.[18] Though the majority of sexual predators are male, up to 25 percent are female.[19] According to a comprehensive study in Canada in 1996, "Mounting research evidence about sexual abuse perpetration at the hands of teen and adult females has begun to challenge our assumptions."[20] The study goes on to report that "the percentage of women and teenage girl perpetrators recorded in case studies is small and ranges from 3% to 10%," and that another study found that female adults were abusers of male victims 37 percent of the time compared to 19 percent for female victims.[21] According to a BBC News program, "Women commit 25% of all child sexual abuse," and 250,000 children in the United Kingdom have been sexually abused by women.[22]

The stereotype of sex-crazed pervert lurking in the shadows is a misconception that needs to be dispelled. According to Marie D. Marth, who works for the Northampton County Adult Probation and Parole, "They are very intelligent, they know how to navigate the Web and hide files on their computers."[23] Some predators want more timely interactions both online and offline and move quickly to meet their online pen pal, often requesting personal phone numbers and addresses or suggesting meeting places within hours or days of conversing online. Others will take a more calculated approach over a longer period of time to gain more trust from their online partner before taking steps that often include swapping photos and email addresses and coordinating a meeting place. Some common definitions that parents need to know include the following.

- **Child pornography:** the illegal use of children in pornographic films or pictures; more recently expanded to include the use of any technology medium and the portrayal of children depicted in an inappropriate sexual manner.
- **Child sexual abuse:** "exposing or subjecting the child to sexual contact, activity, or behavior. Sexual abuse includes oral, anal, genital, buttock, and breast contact. It also includes the use of objects for vaginal or anal penetration, fondling, or sexual stimulation."[24]
- **Child solicitation:** solicitation of a child to engage in sexual conduct. *Solicit* can mean that the conduct (commanding, entreating, or attempting to persuade a specific person) may be accomplished in any manner, including in person, by telephone, by letter, or by computerized or other electronic means.[25]
- **Child exploitation:** exploitation of a minor through video, filming, phone cameras, photographs, or other technical reproduction means depicting sexual acts involving a minor.
- **Pedophile:** According to a Netsmartz article, "A pedophile is a person who has a sexual preference for prepubescent children and fantasizes about having sex with them."[26]

How do sexual predators reach children today? The answer is via a variety of means and technology that usually starts after an online meeting, followed up by a personal one-on-one meeting. Some predators simply abuse their roles in their jobs or as a volunteers and make a personal connection with a minor before attempting to exploit or harm them. Examples of sexual abuse of children not involving technology include abuse of power and interaction with minors by teachers, coaches, priests, baby-sitters, family members, and friends. Avenues for approaching a child online include postings on social networking sites, email, IM, and chat rooms. What I find fascinating about today's wired teens is their willingness to disclose personal information and day-to-day drama to strangers via the Internet or those posing as friends online. I've had many conversations with friends, colleagues, and children over the course of researching this book, and I believe that teens are more trusting of others while online and they don't really understand the mind of an Internet predator, nor the risks of posting personal information for the world to see—especially things that they probably wouldn't tell some of their friends in person. In any case, it is the parents' and teachers' jobs to monitor the children they care about in an effort to protect them from risks they simply don't comprehend or choose to ignore.

In the course of my research on Internet predators, I came across a group that is working hard to help protect children: Perverted Justice (www.perverted-justice.com). They were featured on an *NBC Dateline* television story that exposed some shocking scenarios and discussions with alleged sexual predators, many resulting in convictions after engaging law enforcement officials. The following is an example of a conversation between an online predator and a potential victim. *Caution:* Some of the text below is graphic, but I feel it's necessary to highlight it to help educate parents and teachers of the dangers of children accessing the Internet. Comments in bold highlight sexually graphic approaches sometimes taken by predators or a cunning approach to win over their victim. Comments in brackets highlight any additional comments pertaining to statements in the conversation.

The initial introduction takes place in a chat room where a predator hones in on a child who has posted pictures and personal data on a social networking site. The following conversation is portrayed as a series of private IM conversations after the predator, a 38-year-old man, requests to move the conversation from a public forum to a more private medium with little or no audit trail. In this scenario, the predator is pretending to be a mature young boy trying to lure a younger girl into more adventurous situations.

Day 1, Conversation after School

Predator: nice screen name . . .

Cutegirl666: thanks! It kind of balances me out—the good and the bad.

Predator: we've had some nice conversations in the teen chat room. Good to get out of the crowded space.

Cutegirl666: i guess so.

Predator: did you just get out of school?

Cutegirl666: yep. kinda sucks . . . i'm sooooo bored.

Predator: where are you now?

Cutegirl666: at home.

Predator: do you ride the bus to school? [an attempt to find out if she is unsupervised during her day]

Cutegirl666: nah . . . I walk. It's pretty close.

Predator: are your parents home too?

Cutegirl666: no. still at work. always working . . .

Predator: gotta pay the bills . . . what are you doing tonight?

Cutegirl666: don't know. maybe watch a movie or chat online again . . .

Predator: oh? Well, how old are you?

Cutegirl666: i'm turning 13 in 3 months. can't wait—maybe my parents will take me seriously then . . .

Predator: I see. do they treat you like a kid now?

Cutegirl666: yeah. I'm the youngest and they don't seem to have time for me.

Predator: where do you live?

Cutegirl666: Boston. [he already knows that from a prior conversation in a chat room]

Predator: I live just outside . . . if your parents don't pay attention to you then you can pretty much do what you want then. right?

Cutegirl666: sometimes. they wouldn't know anyway. I could runaway and they probably wouldn't find out for days.

Predator: too bad you aren't older—like 17 . . .

Cutegirl666: why? do you like older women? LOL . . .

Predator: not really, just girls that are more mature or like to try new things . . .

Cutegirl666: like what? The 666 in my name isn't there for no reason.

Predator: I don't know. Ever play spin the bottle or 30 seconds in a closet?

Cutegirl666: yeah, but I had to kiss this really ugly geek guy.

Predator: I'm not a geek . . . and I kinda like girls that can be my best friend and spend time hugging and kissing . . .

Cutegirl666: I can do that . . . but only for the right guy, ya know?

Predator: yeah I know. I've had a few girlfriends, but am still looking for one that can go beyond my good looks . . .

Cutegirl666: so you're hot!!!

Predator: I don't know. I think i'm kinda normal, but all the girls tell me i'm cute.

Cutegirl666: send me a picture.

Predator: ok, but don't laugh . . . It was taken when I was 16. [outright lie]

Cutegirl666: ok . . . i'll send you one of mine and we'll compare. let's rate each other.

Predator: be nice . . . i'm sure you're really pretty. you seem very nice online and i love talking to you. let's talk again tomorrow . . .

Cutegirl666: ok, but send me your photo via IM. [predators prefer using tools like IM to send files because they don't usually leave an audit trail of the transfer like email would]

In this case, the predator would likely send a photo of an attractive 17-year-old boy in an attempt to lure her in for a meeting. At this point, he changes gears and starts a discussion about sexual experiences.

Day 3: After Several Days of Trivial Conversations and Getting to Know Each Other

Predator: ok. let's play truth or dare . . . [time to find out how playful she may be, hoping she selects dare]

Cutegirl666: ok. dare.

Predator: I dare you to take off your top and run to the mailbox and back . . .

Cutegirl666: serious????

Predator: chicken. afraid somebody else is going to see that cute body of yours? I put your picture above my computer so that I can see you while we chat . . .

Cutegirl666: oh . . . don't call me a chicken. you just wait until it's my turn. be right back . . .

Predator: wish I had a video camera for this . . . funny stuff.

Cutegirl666: i'm back!!!! i think the old guy down the street saw me . . . that was fun . . . my turn.

Predator: how long did it take you?

Cutegirl666: once i took my top off—30 seconds. i'm really fast.

Predator: fast in what way?

Cutegirl666: running stupid . . .

Cutegirl666: my turn: truth or dare?

Predator: truth.

Cutegirl666: how far have you gone?

Predator: you mean???

Cutegirl666: yes.

Predator: round the bases . . . it's a rush, but only with girls that I really like. have you done it yet? [trying to determine sexual experience]

Cutegirl666: kinda.

Predator: kinda. it's really a yes or no answer. it's alright if you're waiting for the right guy. I don't blame you, but it really feels great when you connect with someone you really like . . .

Cutegirl666: ok, so not all the way but close . . .

Predator: how close?

Cutegirl666: i'm afraid of going all the way . . . one of my friend tells me it hurts. i like giving BJs instead . . .

Predator: ok, nothing to be afraid of. maybe i can help . . .

Cutegirl666: what??? you serious? what kinda tips can you give me?

Predator: i'm serious . . . we seem to hit it off well. Let's meet and get to know each other. you never know . . . i could be gentle with you . . .

Cutegirl666: that's funny. i would like to meet you though.

Predator: glad to hear that. I can't get the image of you running down the driveway with your minis bouncing in the wind . . .

Cutegirl666: you crack me up. they're not that big—but they're growing . . . LOL.

Predator: I think your really nice and hot too . . .

Cutegirl666: I think you're cute . . .

At this point, he changes his tone to be more sexual, then backs off a bit and reintroduces the idea of meeting.

Predator: are your parents home?

Cutegirl666: no, why?

Predator: I'd like to hear what your voice sounds like . . . i have a feeling you have a sexy voice for your age . . .

Cutegirl666: hah! you wish. what do you sound like? young boy or old man?

Predator: nice boy silly . . . Do you know how to make a recording to an audio file?

Cutegirl666: no . . .

Predator: I could teach you or if it's easier just call you? Is there a phone number where I can reach you that only goes to you—like a cell phone? [predators usually look for ways to reach out that don't involve parents and can't be tracked easily]

Cutegirl666: yes. my dad let's me have a cell phone to keep touch with me since he's always working or traveling for his job . . . My cell is 617-xxx-xxxx. What's your phone number?

Predator: I'll just call you. hang on . . .

Cutegirl666: ok . . . getting jittery . . .

Predator: All around? tits perky too?

Cutegirl666: serious? Yeah—a bit of that too . . .

Predator: cool . . . Do you have small or big nipples? I'm calling you now.

He dials a prefix to prevent caller ID from displaying his number and pretends to be a older teenager. After the call, he resumes online.

Cutegirl666: you sound older than 17 . . .

Predator: Nope . . . just have a deep voice. girls at school tell me it's sexy . . .

Cutegirl666: do you have a girlfriend?

Predator: nope, but i'd like one. your voice is sexy . . . maybe we can spend some time together and get more mature???

Cutegirl666: ahh . . . the teacher in you again. wait your turn . . . in good time.

Predator: so, maybe you'll let me see a little more than that photo you sent me? how about a quick PC video-cam flash? do you have one?

Cutegirl666: no. dad thinks it's too risky for me . . . he's right!!!!!

Predator: ok. can I ask you a personal question since you're hot and all???

Cutegirl666: okay.

Predator: what color underwear do you have on now?

Cutegirl666: I'm not wearing any . . .

Predator: nice.

Cutegirl666: i'm kidding . . . i have on red and white ones . . .

Predator: what are they covering up? anything interesting???

Cutegirl666: like what? if i'm a guy or a girl . . . LOL

Predator: no, you know what I mean . . . do you have any hair? [some sexual predators that prey on young girls are fanatic about clean or shaven genitals]

Cutegirl666: that's funny . . . yes, why?

Predator: don't know. seems like the older girls are big into shaving. kinda looks sexy that way. would you ever try it? [an attempt to get her to try and act more mature and do things more mature women would do; a common approach by predators]

Cutegirl666: ooouuucchhh! i'd probably cut myself and bleed all over the floor . . . that's gross.

Predator: it's not that bad. check out the following site to see what i mean . . . [he gives her an address to a teen Web site that shows naked girls engaged in a variety of risqué poses]

Cutegirl666: this i gotta see . . . hold on while i bring up the site . . . that's pretty freaky!!!! some of those girls look like their my age! do you look at sites like this a lot???

Predator: nah . . . one of my friends told me about it. my last girlfriend was *clean* shaven though . . . it's pretty sexy. you should give it a try. try clipping first, then using some cream . . .

Cutegirl666: you serious??? pervert!!!

Predator: ok, so don't try it. I'm not a PV . . . the older girls are mature about this kinda stuff. maybe i thought you could handle it . . . [coercion attempt]

Cutegirl666: maybe I can. I think i'm mature for my age . . .

Predator: prove it. [capitalizing on his prior approach for a dare]

Cutegirl666: ok . . . ok, maybe i'll give it a try . . .

Predator: that's my girl . . . we should get together soon in person . . . how about thursday after school?

Cutegirl666: i can't. i'm studying with a friend of mine. how about next week?

Predator: what day? can't wait to meet you and start the process of making you into an older woman! like shaving . . . maybe we can start you on a six-step program and shake those fears of having sex quickly . . .

Cutegirl666: easy romeo . . . in due time . . .

Predator: so i have a chance? cool . . . would love to be your first . . . you seem special to me . . . i promise i'll be gentle when I fuck you!!! i don't like to wear condoms—hope you don't mind . . . [sexual predators often jump in and out of graphic conversations as a mechanism to test the waters and gauge a reaction]

Cutegirl666: what?

Predator: just kidding . . . can't you take a joke?

Cutegirl666: yeah, but that's just rude . . . i prefer to call it *making love*. that's what my mom tells me . . .

Predator: here we go again. I thought you told me you had a little 666 in you? seriously, all kidding aside, I'd love to meet you in person and get to know you. maybe catch a movie or something?

Cutegirl666: that sounds like fun.

Predator: can you meet me outside the library on 7th and Maple about a mile from your school on monday at 7 pm?

Cutegirl666: why so late and in the dark?

Predator: i have to do something with my brother before . . . maybe we can go to a movie at 8 and get to know each other . . . [darkness allows him a lot of options, which include kidnapping. Many sexual encounters have occurred after a brief kidnapping, resulting in a sexual assault, possibly in the car or at a nearby location. Some predators keep their victims for days and even weeks, sometimes sexually torturing them. Others drop off their victims at another location after the initial assault.]

Cutegirl666: sounds like fun. let me ask my mom later . . .

Predator: no parents!!! just figure out a way to get away . . . kinda like a romantic first meeting . . . I'm getting jittery now . . .

Cutegirl666: i'm kinda excited about meeting you too. ok. i'll tell my mom i'm going to a friend's house to study. don't know about a movie. it depends on how my mom reacts before i leave . . .

Predator: ok. can't wait to meet you in person. I'll be in a hot dark blue mustang! my older brother lets me borrow his car every once in a while . . .

Cutegirl666: wow—hot!!! hope you're as hot as that car stud . . .

Predator: you'll see . . . see you monday. I'll call you on your cell phone at 6 pm that day to make sure you can make it. make sure your parents don't see you take the call or they'll never let you go and your shot at meeting prince charming will be gone . . .

Cutegirl666: what a drama queen . . . I'll be there.

Predator: don't forget to wear something hot! everyone that sees us will want to be me with the hottie, who's also a nice person . . .

Cutegirl666: really?

Predator: sure. can't wait to see you for our first meeting. remember—don't tell anyone . . . can't wait to see you. chow!

Conversations like these and some even more graphic occur all the time. Children who enter chat rooms, use IM, or maintain a social network page or Web site are at risk. The first step for parents is to ask their children what tools and sites they use and visit. Don't always believe their answers, as children have a propensity to cover up activities that they believe they are mature enough to handle. The next step is to use stealth software, discussed in Chapter 5, to capture their online passwords. Once parents have these passwords, they can explore the sites for content and record online activities like chat conversations to find out what the kids are up to. The Internet can be a scary place, and the only defense for parents and teachers is a solid offense. Sometimes that requires adults to delve into their children's online world in a stealth manner. Parents need to do whatever it takes to keep predators like these and inappropriate content away from their kids. Check the Perverted Justice Web site to look for excerpts from convicted offenders.

Blogs and Social Networking

Blogging is essentially just an online diary posted onto a Web site. It's a catchphrase that's gotten a lot of traction in the last year or so and is popular with the younger generation. Sexual predators, including older ones, have adjusted quickly to be able to understand social networking sites like MySpace and Friendster to prey on others. MySpace and other sites have many benefits, but they come with some risks, including providing teens (and children posing as teens) with an online avenue for expressing themselves. Chapter 4 provides several examples of some real-world tragedies that have taken place as a result of children exposing too much about themselves or meeting the wrong person online.

Text Messaging via Cell Phones

Text messaging is another popular medium for online communication, one that has exploded across the globe as inexpensive cell phones have proliferated. In some countries that have stricter cultures that prohibit unmarried teens of the opposite sex to engage in personal meetings, text messaging is an alternative way to communicate even across very short distances, like café seats or in cars. Many phone vendors bundle text messaging services as part of the monthly bill at no additional cost, whereas others charge a small fee per message sent. These charges can add up quickly with actively texting teens, so check the bills to see just how often your child is on a cell phone and then determine if you need to monitor and review the activity. Call your cell phone provider and asking them for the best way to review text content being sent and received over their service.

Where teens often make mistakes regarding text messaging is by giving out their phone number or starting an online conversation with someone that they don't know and disclosing personal information such as full name, address, school, and so on. Online predators are quite effective at exposing information and using small pieces of personal data to gain more information. Chapter 4 exposes some tragedies involving text messaging and phones that are unfortunate but well worth the read.

PDAs

PDAs, personal digital assistants, are devices that evolved from cell phones and include additional features beyond making voice calls. Common features in PDAs include voice calls and voicemail, text messaging, IM clients, a built-in Internet browser, a calendar, contact list, notes section, and memo pad. PDAs come from a variety of vendors including BlackBerry, Microsoft, Hewlett Packard, Sony, and Palm. What's interesting about these devices are the features they have, the continually falling cost, and their adoption by teens. Teens use these devices as they gain adoption by their parents, teachers, and other professionals, which facilitates acceptance by adults who end up purchasing them for their children.

The risks of using PDAs is that they can complicate a parent's ability to protect a child and monitor online activity because they are decentralized and not connected to computers. That makes it harder to control their use, monitor what software has been installed on them, and review the people and sites that their children visit while using them. I carry a sophisticated BlackBerry and couldn't do without it for work and personal life. However, my wife has no knowledge of what I do with it or what Web sites I access with it—reaffirming just how difficult is to for an adult to manage these small devices. Most Web sites that people visit or messages sent are not recorded or reviewed by employers or parents. Parents who decide to let their teen have one of these multifeatured devices should consult with their provider (examples: T-Mobile, AT&T, etc.) for assistance in getting reports of online usage. Everything is usually logged at the provider, and provided to law enforcement if subpoenaed, but not kept forever due to the cost of storing information on servers and disk systems.

SOME STATISTICS FOR KIDS GOING ONLINE

There are a number of excellent published studies that examine teen use and risks on the Internet along with safety statistics. I highlight three reports here that offer up some humbling and scary realities associated with today's wired youth.

Netsmartz

The NetSmartz Workshop is a great resource from the National Center for Missing and Exploited Children (NCMEC) and Boys & Girls Clubs of America (BGCA).[27] Here are some of their data.

- 61 percent of 13- to 17-year-olds have a profile page on a social networking site.
- 71 percent have received messages online from someone that they did not know.
- 45 percent have been asked to give out personal information by people they did not know.
- 30 percent have considered meeting a person that they've met online.
- 14 percent have actually met people they've met online (9 percent of 13–15-year-olds, 22 percent of 16- and 17-year-olds).[28]

National Center for Missing and Exploited Children (NCMEC)

NCMEC, established in 1984, helps prevent child abduction and sexual exploitation, helps find missing children, and assists victims.[29] In addition to operating the CyberTipline, it serves as a clearinghouse for information about missing and exploited kids.[30] According to a 2000 NCMEC study of 1,501 minors who regularly use the Internet,

- 1 in 33 teens surveyed received aggressive sexual solicitation from a person that asked to meet them somewhere.
- 1 in 17 was threatened or harassed.
- 25 percent of those who received a sexual solicitation actually told their parents.
- 33 percent of parents surveyed with home computers indicated that they had Internet filtering software installed to help protect their children.
- Girls were twice as likely as boys for sexual solicitations at 66 percent versus 34 percent.
- Younger teens (aged 10 to 13) were more likely to be distressed than older children, suggesting that the younger set has a harder time getting past unwanted solicitations.
- Just over 66 percent of solicitors were reported as males compared to 25 percent from females.
- 70 percent of youth surveyed reported that they were at home when sexually solicited online compared to 22 percent at someone else's house.[31]

A sampling of some scary testimony from youth in the NCMEC report turns up the following.

- A 13-year-old girl was asked her bra size.
- A 12-year-old girl indicated that her online contacts described sexual activity they were doing and asked her to masturbate.
- A 13-year-old boy indicated that a female asked him how big his private area was and wanted him to masturbate to completion.[32]

The Exposure of Youth to Unwanted Sexual Material on the Internet: A National Survey of Risk, Impact, and Prevention

The University of New Hampshire published a study in 2003 that surveyed over 1,000 youths (796 boys and 705 girls), 10- to 17-year-olds, and their caretakers. The following provides some interesting highlights that support risks outlined in this chapter.

- 25 percent of youth reported at least one unwanted exposure to sexual pictures while online in the previous year.
- 73 percent of such exposures happened while surfing or browsing the In-

ternet, and 27 percent occurred while reading email or clicking on links provided through IM conversations.

- 67 percent of the incidents happened at home, but 15 percent happened in school, 13 percent at someone else's home, and 3 percent in a library.
- 32 percent of images displayed showed people having sex, and 7 percent of those involved violence in addition to the nudity.
- 92 percent of email exposure came from unknown senders.
- Boys encountered more unwanted sexual material (57 percent) than girls (42 percent).
- Older youth (15 or older) were more exposed (60 percent) than younger youth.
- Troubled youths who reported physical, sexual abuse, or depression had more exposure.[33]

Needless to say, there is plenty of research to support the need for parents and educators to take a more proactive approach in helping protect today's minors and tomorrow's leaders from some of the tremendous risks online.

HOW ARE PARENTS DOING PROTECTING THEIR KIDS?

Before jumping into an overview of the tools that kids use to access the Internet, take a look at the results of two parental surveys gauging how well parents are doing to protect children.

Parents' Internet Monitoring Study

Cox Communications, NCMEC, and Netsmartz.org conducted a study of 503 parents and teens (between 13 and 17) in February 2005 who had Internet access from home. Below are the key findings.

- The highest placement of home computers that had access to the Internet was in the family room (34 percent), followed by the bedroom (30 percent).
- 51 percent of parents do not have software or do not know if software is installed on their home computers to monitor what their children do on the Internet.
- Of the 49 percent that do use software to monitor their children, 87 percent review their children's activities, with 23 percent reporting daily and 33 percent reporting monthly at best.

- 61 percent of parents report that their teenagers use chat rooms and IM tools.
- 42 percent of parents do not review what their teenagers read or write in chat rooms or via IM.
- 96 percent of parents were unable to identify the meaning of P911 as parent alert, and 92 percent were unable to identify what A/S/L (age, sex, location) meant in IM lingo.[34]

Smith Survey of Child Internet Usage and Parental Protection

I ran an anonymous survey of 100 parents in the United States that have children between the ages of 8 and 17. I intentionally expanded the age bracket for my survey to include children below the age of 10, because I've seen elementary school children using computers at school and home in the past few years. I also intentionally asked specific questions as to how and with what tools parents use to monitor or block inappropriate content. The results from this survey are staggering, especially for young children, and clearly demonstrate that parents are clueless with regard to the risks of going online and how to really monitor and protect their children. See for yourself in Table 3.2.

The overall results of my survey were mainly consistent with results from other large-scale surveys. What my survey revealed is that parents think that looking over their kid's shoulder periodically or placing the computer in a common area in the house is effective monitoring. In addition, although the use of Internet Explorer Content Advisor is well intentioned, it rarely stops a technology-savvy teenager, who can simply do one of the following to bypass its controls.

- Dodge the Content Advisor's limits. Many parents that I've spoken to who use IE Content Advisor check the adult content box as their only method of using technology to prevent inappropriate content. The IE Content Advisor allows for the following categories to be managed: language, nudity, sex, and violence. It doesn't allow a more sophisticated set of restrictions that other software packages have. Most teens will still be able to access social networking, chat, IM, and so on with the way most parents use IE Content Advisor.
- Guess the password and bypass it. Once this is done, one can regularly delete temporary Internet files (cache), cookies, and history to cover one's tracks. My own children have become quite adept at guessing passwords, which is why we change them frequently and suspend their online activities for a period of time if we catch them at it.

Table 3.2 Smith Poll Results

Q1. Do your children under the age of 18 have access to the Internet or other related Internet technologies? Examples include: (a) Web browsing, (b) phone text messaging, (c) email accounts, (d) instant messaging accounts, (e) personal digital assistants (PDAs) with text messaging.

Yes: 96 percent

No: 4 percent

Q2. What ages are your children with online access? Results listed averages in order from youngest to oldest for families with multiple children.

1. Child #1: 11.6 years old
2. Child #2: 10.6 years old
3. Child #3: 10.3 years old
4. Child #4: 12 years old

Interestingly enough, I also tracked the oldest and youngest child with Internet access. Surprisingly, the youngest child was at age 4 and the oldest was 17. Several parents indicated other younger children as well, which included 5–7-year-olds.

Q3. Do you think that the Internet poses any risks to children today?

Yes: 98 percent

No: 2 percent

Q4. Do you monitor your children' s access to the Internet?

Yes: 95 percent

No: 5 percent

These responses included soft Internet monitoring, such as periodically looking on a computer screen to see what a child is doing. Soft monitoring is not very effective, especially as children get into the teenager years.

Q5. If so, how do you monitor them?

The following answers were most common (in descending order).

1. The computer is in a common room and we check what they are doing regularly. They do not have computers in their bedrooms.
2. I am in the same room with them, always.
3. I sit next to them if they need to respond to an email or if they want to look up something online. They use browsers such as askforkids.com, kidsclick.com, and yahooligans.com to filter out some of the questionable material online.
4. Walk in on them when they are using it. Question them about what they are going online for, and then "spot check" the usage.
5. All emails received are forwarded to my personal email as well.
6. Through the use of CyberSitter and by looking at logs created by IE and CyberSitter. I get a daily email on all IM activity.
7. Content filters in the IE browser.

The following answers were less common.

1. Keylogger software, computer placement (in the middle of the family room), time limits, and parental control software.
2. Parental blockers and email checks.

Table 3.2 *(continued)*

3. I have AOL, which has very good parental controls. They block sites that are inappropriate and as the parent you can block any additional things you find inappropriate. At the end of the day they will send you an email that lets you know the Web sites that they successfully visited, and the ones that were blocked. They also tell you how many people they IM with and how many email messages were sent and received. I can set the limit for how long they are allowed daily on the Internet, and I have blocked complete access to chat rooms.

To complete this section, an interesting and very personal response.

Rule # 1: An adult must be present while my daughter is on the computer. Moreover, I have tried very hard to instill good Christian values in my children and ask them to follow the 10 commandments in all aspects of their life. I am, however, not naive enough to believe these standards will not be tested by the most cunning and conniving of individuals who continue to infest our society through their lack of respect for life and God's divine will. It is a sick world we live in and only a parent's presence can keep a child safe!

Q6. What age did you allow your children to access the following technologies?

	Low Average Response (for those with access)	Average Age Response (for those with access)	High Age Response (for those with access)
Note: 0 was entered where children didn't have access.			
1. Internet/Web page browsing	4	8.8	15
2. Email accounts	4	9.6	15
3. Cell phones without text messaging	7	12.2	16
4. Cell phones with text messaging	10	13.6	16
5. Instant messaging accounts	8	11.4	16
6. Accounts on social networking sites/Web blogs (like MySpace)	10	14.2	17

Q7. What' s the most common reason you allow your children to access the Internet or other related online technologies?

1. Peer pressure—other kids have access	3 percent
2. School work and projects	68 percent
3. To stay in contact with me—I work	0 percent
4. They're good kids and I trust them	18 percent
5. Other	11 percent

Q8. Do you block or filter Internet sites or pages for your children?

Yes: 39 percent

No: 61 percent

Note: These numbers are in line with other studies done, where parents are asked if they use specific software to help block objectionable content, sites, or services such as IM and online chat.

(continued)

Table 3.2 *(continued)*

Q9. If so, what is the primary tool(s) that you use to block or filter Internet content for your children? The following answers were most common among responses listed of the parents that did employ software for safety in descending order.
1. Internet Explorer Content Advisor (lead choice by 2:1 of any other option)
2. AOL Parental Controls
3. CyberSitter
4. SurfPatrol
5. Norton Internet Security
6. Not sure of the name, my husband installed it
7. Earthlink Parental Controls
8. SafeEyes
9. KidsWatch

One final interesting response: I tried to block Runescape, but they figured it out and unblocked it. Other than that, I don't worry and don't block because I trust them.

Q10. Do you know anyone whose children (17 or under) were harmed emotionally or physically by using or accessing the Internet?
Yes: 22 percent
No: 78 percent

- Install another browser and hide it from the Desktop. Favorites include Firefox and Netscape. IE controls simply don't work on these browsers, and they can gain access to any site or service they want.
- Use a proxy site that masks where minors go online. Once connected to a proxy site, future Web pages viewed through the site are hard to log and monitor, thus camouflaging the real destinations many teens use on the Internet. Sophisticated Internet filtering software can block access to these sites and remove the risk.
- Borrow a neighbor's wireless Internet service and bypass any firewall restrictions put in place at their own home. A wireless network card is needed to dodge controls in this manner.

I found it fascinating that parents allowed very young children to browse the Internet, have email accounts, and use IM tools. These parents may be too lenient with their children's access to the Web, and perhaps they don't fully understand the risks. Hopefully, after reading this chapter along with Chapter 4, parents will begin to rein in some of those privileges and establish some real monitoring that involves using more sophisticated software (discussed in Chapter 5).

I found that the average age for kids using social networking sites, just over

14, was a bit young, because most sites only allow those 14 and older to register. I also found it interesting that the parents were able to say with almost complete certainty that their children did or did not use email, IM, and social networking sites. With 61 percent of respondents indicating that they did not use software to filter or monitor their children's online activities, how would they know if the kids have a Web mail account, use IM, or have posted personal information to a social networking site? Without logging software, the only thing they have to go on is their own two eyes.

I was also surprised at the larger response than anticipated (22 percent indicated yes) to the question, "Do you know anyone whose children (17 or under) that were harmed emotionally or physically by using or accessing the Internet?" I was expecting the number to be smaller. This may indicate that there are a larger set of minors than I anticipated that have been harmed emotionally or physically by going online. I would like to see larger national polls explore this question to see the impact on a larger sample size before drawing any formal conclusions.

PROTECTION AT SCHOOL AND IN LIBRARIES

Although schools and libraries have made great progress to help protect minors on the Internet, they have a long way to go. Two specific laws in the United States have made some progress with regard to protecting minors. The Children's Online Privacy Protection Act (COPPA) of 1998 was drafted to prevent online services and Web sites from collecting personal information from a child as defined by the law as an individual under the age of 13.[35] The Children's Internet Protection Act (CIPA), signed into law in December 2000, requires schools that use certain federal funds and E-rate discounts to have an Internet safety policy and provide technology to protect and shield children and adults from unacceptable content, including visual deceptions that are obscene, harmful to minors, or contain child pornography.[36] Other countries have similar laws and have passed a number of statutes intended to protect minors and prosecute those who abuse them. CIPA requires certain schools to establish policies and software protection. However, there is no standard for what software protection is taken. Simply put, some schools use better Internet filtering and monitoring solutions than others, exposing some children to additional risks.

To prove my point, I ran a series of tests in November 2006 at a large public school system with the following profile: over 100,000 students, over 150 schools in the county, over 15,000 employees. The school system had Internet policies and software installed throughout the county. I conducted my test using a second-grade user account. The following reveals what I was and was not able to do while accessing the Internet during that test.

Successfully Accessed

- Accessed Google and changed the safe surfing settings from moderate filter to none. This setting saves preferences on the local computer and impacts search results greatly.
- Searched for *sex*, resulting in 415 million page links returned.
- Accessed many graphic sexual images via the Google Images tab after page results were returned.
- Viewed a homemade video posted on the Internet (one of the resulting links returned from the Google search) of two adults having sex in their kitchen.
- Downloaded another browser program (Netscape).
- Accessed personal/consumer email Web pages (e.g., MSN mail).

Unsuccessful Attempts

- Was not able to access several adult content sites by name (e.g., www.playboy.com).
- Could not access Web sites commonly used to mask online use.
- Could not remove programs that were installed on the computer.
- Was not able to alter programs listed on the Start menu within the operating system.
- Could not access a command line window to enter operating system or program commands manually.

Private school systems often have Internet protection in place, but again they vary in the quality of those tools and staff supporting them, mainly due to costs. The wealthiest schools can thus afford to have better protection, but only if the support staff or outsourced systems professionals are engaged to provide that protection. At one private school that I visited, monitoring software was in place to detect what sites and services (IM, VOIP, etc.) kids were using, but they didn't actually block access to those sites or services.

Public libraries in the United States offer another area for children and predators alike to view inappropriate content or simply communicate via online tools, many of them encrypted to hide the online conversation from library attendants. I visited a public library in Maryland and found the following rules and circumstances.

- The library maintains access to the Internet as a matter of policy grounded in the First Amendment and existing laws.
- Users must have a library card, must have a PIN, and sign up to use a computer that has Internet access.
- Customers are expected to be considerate of others when viewing material online and, if necessary, use a privacy screen to view certain content and materials that children shouldn't see.
- Library staff may call the police if they believe that a customer is printing, downloading, emailing, or distributing child pornography on their systems.
- Computers in the children's section of the library are equipped with filtering software to prevent viewing inappropriate content.
- The library contained computers with unfiltered access to the Internet and recommends using search engine filters to filter content.

Thus, as long as an individual is being discreet, is not engaged in viewing or distributing child pornography, and complies with state laws to prevent viewing of mature content by minors, they can access pretty much anything they want. This is perhaps not a great place to turn your teen loose.

RECOMMENDATIONS

The risks associated with going online are real, and most children can't (or refuse to) recognize the problems of what has become a very open and socially online population facilitated by content growth technological innovation, making it easy and fun to communicate online. Parents are encouraged to learn as much as they can about the risks associated with the Internet and how predators are using it to abuse and inflict physical and emotional harm on youth. This book advocates an eight-step plan (see Figure 3.2) designed to mitigate online risks for children. The plan includes the following.

1. Establish computer use policies at home.
2. Maintain administrative passwords for computers in their homes. This includes putting restrictions on what each child account can do, such as install new software.
3. Use safe email programs that include anti-spam protection.

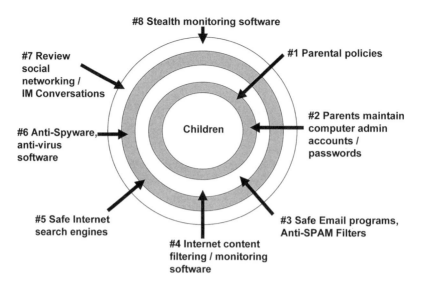

Figure 3.2 Insulating Against the Risks

4. Use Internet content filtering and monitoring software to limit content and programs for children.
6. Use safe Internet search engines or lock down consumer ones.
7. Use anti-spyware and anti-virus programs to protect personal data.
8. Review social networking and IM conversations.
9. Using stealth monitoring software to see exactly what your child is doing online

The following recommendations should help parents and educators understand the risks of going online and reporting an incident to the appropriate authority.

1. There are hundreds of good Web sites designed to reinforce the risks of going online and help parents and teachers protect children. The following Web sites are exemplary in both content and approach.

- FBI: www.fbi.gov/hq/cid/cac/crimesmain.htm
- The Pew Internet and American Life Project: www.pewinternet.org
- NetSmartz Workshop: www.netsmartz.org
- Wired Safety, one of the largest online safety sites: www.wiredsafety.org
- The National Center for Missing and Exploited Children: www.missingkids.com

2. The CyberTipline was created to provide a way for people to notify professionals of a specific risk on the Internet or a person that they know is being harassed, potentially exploited, or stalked by an Internet predator. Concerned individuals can either call (800)The-Lost (843–5678) or fill out an online form at www.cybertipline.org to report an incident.

3. Julie Clark and John Walsh have put together a great educational video to help protect children online. For parents with younger children below the age of 12, check out the www.thesafeside.com to purchase a video that creatively educates younger children and their parents of the risks associated with using chat rooms, email, and browsing.

4. For more information on female sexual predators, consult the 45-minute video *When Girls Do It: The Story of Female Sexual Predators*, produced by Vancouver filmmaker Glynis Whiting. The video provides a provocative and compassionate look at the motivations behind women who abuse children and the effects of their crimes on their victims. This film can be ordered from www.nfb.ca, NationalFilmBoardofCanadaInternational@nfb.ca, 1-800-542-2164 (US), or 1-800-267-7710 (Canada).

5. For more information about how some courageous volunteers are fighting the threats of online predators and working with law enforcement officials, visit the www.perverted-justice.com. Beware, some of this site contains graphic content, conversations, and transcripts of conversations with convicted sexual predators.

6. For information about what the FBI is doing to combat and investigate crimes against children, check out their Investigative Programs, Crimes Against Children Web page at www.fbi.gov/hq/cid/cac/crimesmain.htm. This is an excellent resource for parents and teachers and includes listings of federal statutes related to crimes against children as well as direct links to each state's sex offender registry Web site.

7. Get involved at your child's school. Ask school officials questions about the security and tools that they've put in place to protect children. Test their systems using the techniques described in this chapter, and report any weaknesses in their software solutions.

Four

The Risks of Going Online

You cannot go around and keep score. If you keep score on the good things and the bad things, you'll find out that you're a very miserable person. God gave man the ability to forget, which is one of the greatest attributes you have. Because if you remember everything that's happened to you, you generally remember that which is the most unfortunate.

—Hubert H. Humphrey

A SAMPLING OF UNFORTUNATE EVENTS

Although technology is a powerful tool, it can provide an anonymous conduit for children and teenagers to access content that may not be appropriate or, more important, communicate with individuals that may do them harm. I've pointed out several statistics in this text and will highlight more where appropriate. According to the Crimes Against Children Research Center's Youth Internet Safety Survey, "One in five children each year receives a direct e-mail solicitation from a child predator," usually after seeing a picture or a profile page online.[1] Predators looking for sex with minors aren't the only bad thing that can happen by going online. Pornography is a serious problem and has a correlation to child molesters, some of whom kill their victims to hide their actions. According to the New Jersey State Police High-Tech Crime Unit based in Trenton, "53 percent of convicted child molesters admit they used child pornography just prior to sexually abusing a child."[2]

When trying to communicate just what can go wrong if children are left to their own, I find it easiest (but unfortunate) to describe some of the bad events, horrors, crimes, and victims of these modern tragedies. Following is a sampling of things that have and can go wrong as a result of a child interacting with the wrong person online or via content seen on the Internet.

Kacie Woody

On December 3, 2002, 13-year old Kacie Woody, who lived in a small town in Arkansas, was abducted and later killed by an Internet predator while her father, a police officer for the city of Greenbrier, was at work.[3] Shortly after it was discovered that Kacie was missing, several law enforcement agencies in Arkansas along with the FBI were engaged and "in less than 20 hours they had a suspect, a suspect vehicle and had located the predator and Kacie."[4] According to documents, the predator was a 47-year-old man from California posing online as a 17-year-old.[5] "Investigators searched the home computer, found an alias that the predator had been using, and traced him to a motel in Conway."[6] Officers found the young girl, who was shot in the head, in a van inside a storage facility in another town in Arkansas.[7] When law enforcement officers closed in on the abductor, he shot himself.[8]

Christina Long

A 25-year old man from Greenwich, Connecticut, pleaded guilty and was sentenced to 30 years in prison for the death of 13-year-old Christina A. Long of Danbury, Connecticut. The predator, Saul Dos Reis, had met his victim online.[9] "Prosecutors contend Dos Reis strangled Long in his car after the pair had sex at the Danbury Fair Mall, and then he dumped her body in a shallow stream in a secluded Greenwich subdivision."[10] Reis's defense attorneys insisted that the death was an accident.[11] Long allegedly published a Web site that contained frequently used racy screen names and had sex with people she'd met in a variety of chat rooms.[12] According to a Netsmartz.org article, "She was the captain of her school cheerleading squad and an altar girl."[13] You never can tell what kids are up to, which is why I advocate a more aggressive approach to managing technology and using stealth tools to find out what kids really do online before it's too late.

A British Minor

A 12-year-old girl vanished for a while to meet a 31-year-old man she met on the Internet.[14] According to the Netsmartz.org recap of the story, the girl had been emailing the man up to five hours per day, and they were planning to meet in Paris.[14] As the investigation unwound, police allegedly found sexual digital photos of children on the alleged predator's computer as well as "sexual allegations involving two underage girls in the U.S."[16] Authorities also found records on his computer indicating that he clearly knew she was underage even though he claimed she lied about her age and said that she was 19.[17] Her parents may have been aware of the massive amount of time the young girl spent on the Internet and may have positioned their computer in a common area in their home and talked with her about not giving out personal information to strangers online.[18] The article concludes with the following statement and advice: "Allowing a child unmonitored access to the Internet is like putting him or her out on a street corner and not watching what happens."[19]

Assault Cases

A 13-year-old girl in Georgia was raped by a man she had met during an online conversation.[20] According to investigators, her alleged predator, a 40-year-old man, pretended to be 17 years old while chatting online.[21] After getting her address, the man attacked and raped her in her home after posing as a repairman to gain access.[22]

Another 13-year-old girl in Minnesota met her alleged sexual predator in a chat room, and the online chat moved to a telephone call, through which they agreed to meet in person.[23] The girl told police that she was taken to a hotel room, raped, and then driven home by her assailant.[24]

Triple Threat Abuse

In 2001, James Warren, age 41, Beth Loschin, age 46, and Michael Montez, age 35, were arrested on multiple charges related to an alleged kidnapping and sexual assault of a 15-year-old girl.[24] The girl, who had been exchanging messages online for several months with Warren, agreed to meet him at a mall where she worked, and she told him that she wanted to run away.[26] The girl told police that within a short period of time after meeting Warren and Loschin, she was "handcuffed much of the time and kept under constant surveillance," and that she'd been sexually assaulted by all three of the adults.[27] According to the USA Today article, Loschin and Warren were arrested. Loschin was charged with sodomy and sexual abuse, and Warren and Montez were charged with kidnapping, sodomy, rape, and sexual abuse.[28]

Webcam Minister

Simon Thomas, a 44-year-old minister with the United Reformed Church in Hythe, Hampshire, England, and a married man with several children, pleaded guilty to 35 charges, including two offenses of raping an 11-year-old boy.[29] An investigation revealed that Thomas had been contacting young boys over Internet chat rooms and telling them to perform sex acts over Webcams.[30] Police found a schedule of over 1,000 names of individuals he had met on the Internet on computers seized from his home, with just under 100 that were under the age of 16.[31] A court hearing revealed that Thomas also exposed himself to several boys over the Internet via Webcams and had arranged to meet four of the boys in town, where he took them to quiet locations and abused them.[32] Thomas was given a sex offender prevention order, banning him from communicating with children.[33]

Julie Doe

A 14-year-old teen, dubbed Julie Doe, and her mother filed a $30 million lawsuit against MySpace after she claimed to be sexually assaulted by a 19-year-old Texas college student.[34] In an interesting twist to this case, the defense attorney for the male student is considering suing MySpace because he says the alleged victim portrayed herself on the social networking site as older than her actual age.[35] According to a *Time* article, the girl set up a MySpace profile in 2005 when she was 13, even though the Web site's rules prohibit accounts for children under 14.[36] Once online, she met the male student, exchanged emails for over a month, exchanged phone numbers, and agreed to meet in person, where he allegedly sexually assaulted her.[37]

Ryan Adams

Ryan M. Adams, 20 years old, was accused of having sex with two boys he met on the Internet and was indicted on six counts of statutory rape of a 14- and 15-year-old boy that he met on MySpace.[38] MySpace and other popular social networking sites are common online venues for Internet predators, and they often represent themselves as another persona.

Supalover666

Police allegations revealed that a 21-year-old man from Kingston, Ontario, built an online environment in which children were groomed for sex.[39] Supalover666, the online screen name (or handle) of Mark Bedford, was allegedly used to enter online chat rooms and look for young girls.[40] Police claim that Bedford tried a variety of things to connect with teens, ranging from looking for interests in sports, music, and dancing or, as a last resort, hacking into their email accounts to gain access to their online buddy lists.[41] According to police, girls as young as nine were "threatened with rape, bodily harm, and even death if they failed to co-operate and perform sex acts on their webcams."[42] According to Ontario Police Detective Sergeant Frank Goldschmidt, who led the nine-month investigation, "I have never seen this many victims involved and it's safe to say that, in this early stage of this investigation, we're looking at well in excess of 100."[43] Bedford allegedly also threatened to post images of his online encounters on Web sites and show them to family members if they refused his requests.[44] Bedford was charged with two counts of luring a child by means of a computer, two counts of possessing child pornography, three counts of making child pornography, two counts of distributing child pornography, and three counts of extortion.[45]

In a related case, 21-year-old Lee Costi was jailed after contacting a 13-year-old girl via a chat room and convincing her to perform sex acts for him over a Web camera.[46] According to the girl, "He kept saying how beautiful I was."[47] Police found over 350 logs of online conversations with young girls on Costi's computer, including conversations with other pedophiles around the world.[48] Costi admitted to three counts of sex with children, three counts of Internet child grooming, and five counts of creating indecent images of children.[49]

A Swedish Case

A 36-year-old Stockholm man was taken into custody on suspicion of raping three young girls after allegedly contacting them via the Internet on a popular youth Web site.[5] The girls, aged 14 and 15, tipped off the police, alleging that the man had raped them, and two indicated they had been forced to have sex with him.[51] The attacks allegedly took place in the man's home, at his work in the city, and at the home of one of the girls.[52] Swedish law states that sex with a minor under the age of 15 is rape, regardless of consent.[53]

Jose Marino

Thirty-six-year old Jose A. Merino was charged with three counts of rape of a child, six counts of sodomy on a child, and four counts of sexual abuse of a child.[54] Police believe he posted a profile on MySpace and posed as a 16-year-old to lure young girls for sexual encounters.[55]

Jacobo Rivera

Thirty-two-year-old Jacobo Rivera of Orem, Utah, agreed to two federal counts of possession of child pornography and faced state other charges, including seven first-degree felony counts of sodomy on a child, rape of a child, and aggravated sex abuse of a child.[56] Rivera's girlfriend at the time discovered pictures on his cell phone of her niece and two daughters and notified police, who arrested him.[57] Because the photos were created on a cell phone, he was also charged with five federal felony counts of production of child pornography.[58]

Online Blackmailing

Two girls, then 13 and 15 years old, went to police to expose an Internet sicko who was preying on them.[59] Their ordeal started when they received an email from a man posing as their friend, which led to a prank flash exposure via a Webcam after conversing in a chat room.[60] They quickly received a message stating, "I'm not who you think I am," followed up by several requests and threats of exposing the pictures to friends, parents, and even posting them to Web sites.[61] An investigator for the case indicated that the alleged predator was suspected of blackmailing over 100 girls on two continents into performing sex acts.[62] The man was subsequently charged with several counts of making and distributing child pornography and extortion.[63]

Joseph Colasacco

Police arrested 30-year-old Joseph Colasacco and charged him with four counts of promoting pornography to a minor, three counts of electronic enticement of a minor, and one count of sexual assault after he was allegedly found in the bed of a 14-year-old boy.[64] According to the prosecutor's spokesperson, the two met on MySpace.[65] According to an affidavit, the boy's mother found pornographic magazines and a DVD in his bedroom "depicting nude men in sexual acts and poses" that according to the boy was brought by Colasacco to his house.[66]

Matthew Gargill

A 29-year-old Hawaiian man was accused of sexually assaulting a 15-year-old girl in his car near a college campus after initially meeting her online.[67] Police say that Matthew Gargill posed as a 16-year-old boy on MySpace and arranged to meet the girl.[68] According to Captain Frank Fuji of the Honolulu Police Department, "The young people using the Internet, you need to realize that if you're being less than truthful about the information you put on the screen, you can be pretty certain that the other people on that screen are probably putting less than truthful information."[69] Officers arrested Cargill for investigation of seven counts of sex assault and one count of electronic enticement of a child.[70]

Paul Bennett

Paul Bennett, 24 years old, was arrested in San Francisco in 2004 and subsequently convicted for transporting a 13-year-old girl across state lines with the intent on engaging in sexual activity.[71] Bennett and the victim met online after a series of email exchanges that led to an Internet romance.[72] The young girl testified that she had sex with Bennett on multiple occasions after leaving League City, Texas, and heading north to Oklahoma, where the pair hitchhiked to California after learning that the FBI was looking for him.[73]

Ronald Elmquist

Radio Shack Corporation reported in November 2006 that its board accepted the resignation of director Ronald Elmquist, who was charged with three counts of possessing child pornography and entered a not guilty plea.[74]

Molesting Son for "Master"

A 38-year-old Canadian woman pleaded guilty to one count of sexual interference with a person under the age of 14 and another count of transmitting child pornography after apparently sending sexual pictures of herself and her 8-year-old son to her master in a bondage-themed online chat room.[76]

Ottawa police also charged Thomas Brian Feehan, 56, with possession of child pornography after seizing his computer from his home.[76] The woman said her master started her submissive training that over time evolved to her using sex toys over a Webcam and eventually to sending him nude pictures of her son touching himself.[77]

RECOMMENDATIONS

This chapter highlights only some of the tragedies that have happened in recent years and will continue to happen in years to come. Part of protecting children and minors from the dangers of the Internet and other technologies is learning just what can go wrong. There are a lot of dangerous people in the world, many of whom inflict harm (sexually, emotionally, physically) on children. Blackmail and tricks to get children to reveal personal details and (sometimes body parts) are commonly used by intelligent predators. Kids need to hear sensitized versions of the events described in this chapter to help better prepare themselves and protect themselves while they are online. The following recommendations close this gruesome reality.

- Have *frequent* conversations with children about the risks of going online, and where appropriate, let them know some of the bad things that have happened to others and how they were duped. I don't advocate a grotesque or detailed account, but children need to know that there are bad people in the world with intent to harm them and how they attempt to do so. I used this approach with my children when I explained why I wouldn't allow them to have an IM account. They're smarter as a result of the conversation and have talked to their friends about some of the risks of going online and communicating with strangers.

- Develop a contract or agreement with your children about things not to do while on the Internet and have them sign it. Reinforce that they should never give out personal information (name, address, phone number, schools, etc.) to anyone they don't know in chat rooms, IM conversations, online games, social networking sites, or email. People aren't always who they say they are.

- Politely explain some of the consequences if they send a photo to a stranger or post one online. Although this seems enticing sometimes, communicate that they shouldn't open picture files sent by strangers. They may be graphic or fake. It's common for Internet predators to send photos of young teens, concealing their real identity and age in an effort to lure them to a personal meeting. Real-world examples of tragedies, if communicated properly, are an excellent way to get a message across to children, especially teenagers, of the potential dangers of going online.

- Set up communication guidelines for conversing with others online, regardless of the medium. These include never responding to rude or inappropriate messages or requests. They should cut off communication with these individuals and inform their parents or teacher immediately. Also, make sure they know that they should *never* agree to meet someone in person that they've met online and reinforce this message with some real-world tragedies that have unfortunately left others as victims, some sexually abused and dead.

PART TWO

A Road Map to Protect Children While Online

How to Monitor Your Kids Online

I've arrived at this outermost edge of my life by my own actions. Where I am is thoroughly unacceptable. Therefore, I must stop doing what I've been doing.
—Alice Koller

TO MONITOR OR NOT TO MONITOR

One thing is for sure when raising children—they will lie at some point. Some lies are minor, but others are more serious. I've watched my kids and others grow up and have noticed the era of "that's my stuff." As children grow into young teenagers, they become more protective of what is theirs and move into a phase of more independence, which includes trying to conceal things from their parents. This chapter discusses three main topics.

1. The types of tricks kids use to hide their online activities
2. Nontechnical parental monitoring
3. Effective technical software to filter and monitor (overt and covert)

TRICKS KIDS USE TO HIDE WHAT THEY'RE DOING

Children with access to the Internet are smarter than we parents give them credit for. My own kids get great grades, play team sports, and are mostly a parent's dream to manage. But they do lie from time to time and on a number of occasions have attempted to get past the software that I've put in place to limit their online activities. (I'm their worst nightmare from a technology stand-point because they'll never surpass my knowledge of computer technology as long as I'm still in the IT profession.) The following list shows some examples of how children use technology to camouflage and hide their online activities.

- *Kids often set up and use multiple email accounts.* When parents monitor their primary email accounts, looking at both sent and received messages, kids may use hidden accounts to send information to their online acquaintances and friends. Stealth software (discussed later in this chapter) will help parents iden-tify those accounts so they can stamp them out and disable them.

- *Teens use a variety of IM tools and sometimes make voice calls over the Internet with these tools.* Parents often lay down the rule that their kids are not allowed to use IM. Rules don't work—technology does. Unless parents use software to block these types of tools at the appropriate age, children can easily misuse them and potentially get into trouble.

- *Technically adept teenagers cover their online browsing tracks by deleting tempo-rary Internet files and recorded history.* It's actually quite easy to do this in most browsers. Microsoft's Internet Explorer now has just one button to click to delete the history, cached temporary Internet files and pages, and data entered into Web page forms. Once the data is gone, parents can't tell where their kids have been on the Web. If you find that this is happening on your home comput-ers, your children may have something to hide.

- *Tech-savvy children often use proxy sites to hide where they're going on the Internet.* These Web pages allow users to enter the Web page that they'd like to go to directly on their site and thus make surfing anonymous and hidden from that point forward. These sites also make it harder for Web logging software to report what sites children have visited. Stealth software fixes that and gives par-ents a true report of Web usage.

- *Teenagers often create personal Web pages on a free service and update content as desired.* Yahoo!'s GeoCities is one such popular service. Teens often publish too much personal content on their personal Web pages, which are available to everyone and often picked up by search engines. Savvy teens can actually turn their home PCs into a Web server by starting a Web publishing service or program. This approach is usually less popular with teens because all of their content is on their home computers and searchable by their parents.

- *Teenagers frequently download and install different browser software, hide the icon from the Desktop, and surf the Internet bypassing content controls in the browser that their parents have set up.* A common example: a parent enables content filtering in Internet Explorer to block adult content. His or her teen downloads Firefox , hides the shortcut icon from the Desktop, and even deletes it from the list of programs on the Application menu, but stores a hidden shortcut in a directory where they can run the program and bypass all IE content filters.

- *Curious children wanting more from the Internet try to crack administrative passwords by watching their parents type on the keyboard.* My own kids have done this a number of times and I type at ninety words a minute! Once a child has an administrative password for a particular computer or Internet content filtering program, they can bypass the controls, setup new accounts, and delete their online tracks and log files. Stealth software and key loggers help mitigate this along with changing administrative passwords on a monthly basis.

- *Teenagers often delete sent and received email and IM messages that they don't want parents to see.* Stealth software reveals exactly what they're trying to hide by capturing screen shots at the desired intervals.

- *Sophisticated teens save private email attachments and downloaded files (pictures, videos, etc.) to data keys (flash drives) instead of the hard drive.* Data keys can store large amounts of information, including full-motion videos of pornography like the infamous Paris Hilton sex frolic. Stealth software reveals all activities on a particular computer, including copying files to data keys.

- *Some teenagers use hot keys to quickly switch between screens and programs when parents walk by the computer.* By pressing the right key combination, kids can bring up a word processing file that looks like a homework assignment in less than a second to conceal what's being accessed via another tool or window.

- *IM- and chat-savvy teenagers use shortcuts and jargon to warn others online when they can no longer converse freely.* These quick phrases and characters are often not known by parents. Some interesting examples include the following. (Chapter 8 provides a detailed list to get parents up to speed.)

- :-*) = kiss
- POS = parent over shoulder
- SA = sibling alert
- IPN = I'm posted naked
- NIFOC = naked in front of the computer
- WTGP? = want to go private?
- KPC = keeping parents clueless
- CTN = can't talk now

- *Teens that want to hide personal IM conversations simply turn off logging within the IM tool itself, leaving no record of the online exchanges.* Email programs by default leave an audit trail, and users must manually delete them to hide the content of the messages. In contrast, IM users only save messages of online conversations to disk on demand. Keep in mind, Internet providers keep a log of content for a period of time, but they usually don't keep them for longer than required by law.

• *Children often change social networking sites frequently and select nonmainstream sites to hide postings from their parents.* In addition, many have profile pages on multiple sites, so if their parents find one and shut it down, they still have another. Given the recent press about social networking sites, most parents already know about MySpace and check to see if their kids have a profile page with inappropriate or personal content posted. They don't usually know about the less advertised alternatives to trendy sites. Internet filtering software that logs Web activity and stealth software that records all activities can help parents find out exactly what sites their kids are posting to. Key loggers also allow adults to capture passwords so they can log in as their child to see their private profile pages. This is not an invasion of privacy. Parents shouldn't feel guilty snooping around and don't need to justify prying to help protect their children. As long as my kids are still minors and living under the roof that I provide for them, they don't have many rights. The privacy advocates can look somewhere else for a discussion on this topic.

• *Smart kids rename files to nondescript names and file types when sending email attachments to prevent parents who monitor their email accounts from viewing them when they try to open the file.* Changing a nude picture file from JPEG to, say, a nonexistent file type like JTT complicates the viewing of such files because the operating system doesn't know what program to launch to see what's inside. An example would be for a teen to rename a file called nakedgirl2.jpeg to hw2.doc or hw2.gss. Most parents wouldn't look into a file that looks like a homework document. To pull off the exchange, the intended recipient simply changes the file extension back, saves it for viewing at a later time (maybe on another computer to a data key), and deletes the email itself. Stealth software exposes these types of tricks and tips off monitoring adults that there may be an issue with online behavior.

Parents and teachers need to learn these types of tricks and start thinking like the opposition to protect children on the Internet today. A tech-savvy parent or teacher with the right tools and techniques can mitigate many of the risks and be at a competitive advantage with their children against the sexual predators that are stalking kids every day.

NONTECHNICAL PARENTAL MONITORING

Although not as effective, the following nontechie approaches to monitoring your kids' activities may help reduce risk, but the recommendation is to employ a technical software solution on every computer in your home and school.

1. Put the family computer in a common room with open access so that it's easy to see what's on the screen.
2. Set time limits for when children can go online, and prohibit them from accessing the Internet when parents or guardians are not home, especially if there isn't any monitoring and filtering software installed.
3. Regularly review what Web sites your child goes to by viewing the browser history.
4. Regularly review your child's sent, deleted, and received emails.
5. If your child has a data key or flash drive, ask to see it from time to time and review the files for inappropriate content.
6. Create sound family policies and agreements of what is acceptable and not acceptable Internet use.

These approaches attempt to reduce the risks associated with using the Internet, but they're not fully effective alone, which is why the remainder of this book is focused on using the right types of technology that do help protect minors that access the Internet. Why take a software approach instead of a more casual approach? Because software doesn't lie and is far more effective at disclosing the truth regarding what children do online. It's also very helpful and more effective at protecting children from inappropriate content and sexual predators. Parents who can see actual conversations between their children and strangers are in a better position to do something about it than those that are in the dark.

SOFTWARE FOR BETTER MONITORING

First I want to clarify the difference between filtering and blocking software. *Filtering* software is usually designed to block access to specific sites containing a series of keywords that are either preprogrammed or keyed in manually. The problem with filtering solutions alone is that Web site operators are pretty smart with regard to misspelling typical keywords. Filters can be used as a set of keywords or combinations of categories such as *adult, drugs, violence*, and so on and turned on or off in most programs. *Blocking* software typically maintains a database of sites by category that, when a filter is set, can block access to those sites. Many companies that offer these solutions employ people to troll the Internet in an attempt to add new sites to the database, keeping the product more current and increasing the effectiveness of the block. As with filtering solutions, the best blocking products also allow parents to add to the bad and good site list. Today's best products employ both strategies—blocking and filtering—and often add components of monitoring or logging as well to help you sift through the data collected when used to monitor online activities.

Filtering and blocking software will still allow the Internet experience to survive and move forward. Given the amount of content and the varying degrees of appropriateness for minors, laws and societies have evolved to institute provisions designed to protect minors while still preserving free speech. Some countries not only filter and block but do it openly, as China regularly does. Saudi Arabia has openly stated that all Internet traffic in and out of the country is routed through a set of central servers that review each Web page requested.[1] If the user's requesting page is on the government's black list or blocked pages, the page is blocked from being viewed by the user.[2]

Browser-based content filters, like Internet Explorer Content Advisor, and search engine parental filter settings are not effective tools for protecting children. Simply put, they don't cut it, especially if children's accounts have rights to install new software or use other nonsecured wireless Internet connections. In addition, Internet-based services that filter and block certain sites and services are not totally effective either. Many who use these services like the functionality and effectiveness, but they don't realize that they can be bypassed. These tools are effective only if their users access the Internet through their provider. Let me be quite honest when I say that the Internet will include many wireless options and providers in the future. It's as easy as tapping into an unsecured wireless connection and using a different browser to bypass many of the online services content filters. Teenagers who have laptop computers with wireless networking cards can simply take their computer to a friend's house, use it at a Starbuck's, or as stated before, tap into another unsecured Internet access point to go where they want on the Internet and download almost anything.

According to a recent U.S. government study, approximately 1.1 percent of Web sites that were searched and indexed by MSN and Google and 1.7 percent of sites indexed by AOL, MSN, and Yahoo! are sexually explicit.[3] In 1998, the U.S. government passed the Child Online Protection Act (COPA), which required commercial Web sites to collect credit card information or other proof of age before allowing users to view material deemed harmful to minors.[4] In 1997, the U.S. Supreme Court deemed portions of the law unconstitutional because they said it was too vague and impacted the free speech rights of adults.[5] In 2004, the Supreme Court blocked COPA and indicated that filtering software may be more effective at protecting children against pornography.[6] According to American Civil Liberties Union attorney Chris Hansen, "COPA—right out of the bat—doesn't block the 50 percent (posted) overseas" and thus "COPA is substantially less than 50 percent effective."[7]

It often takes a very public scandal involving sex or crimes against children to raise awareness of the risks of using the Internet. According to a *Wall Street Journal* article, in the two weeks after the Congressman Mark Foley scandal broke, some sales of monitoring and filtering tools for parents saw double-digit growth.[8] According to Philip B. Stark, a professor at the University of California at Berkley, "Filters are more than 90 percent effective."[9] Does that mean that most software filtering programs are by default 10 percent ineffective? If so, that's already putting them into the B grade, at best, right out of the shrink-wrapped box. I believe that only a few filtering/monitoring software programs are effective, and not many can claim 90 percent effectiveness. Many of the packages I tested failed my images and video tab test when searching for adult content. When they fail, they fail big, often returning very graphic content. We're not just talking about the percentage of successfully blocked pages, we're dealing with the varying degrees of inappropriateness of content returned.

As a result, my recommendation is clear: install the right monitoring/filtering software on all computers, desktops and especially laptops, where children access the Internet. I evaluated a variety of software solutions before coming up with the following recommendations for parents and teachers. As a result, I've selected two software products to help parents and teachers do a better job protecting children on the Internet, regardless of the browser or Internet-based communications tools children use. I used the following criteria. The product must be:

- effective and work as advertised (50 percent weighting)
- easy to set up and use and produce accurate reports (40 percent weighting)
- cost-effective (10 percent weighting)

Cost represented only a small portion of the total weighting when selecting products. As with many other things in life, you get what you pay for. To be effective, a product must not only work as advertised but pass a series of tests. Many products failed my search engine test and displayed graphic sexual photos and videos. At no time during my evaluation of software solutions was I coerced, bribed, given free software, or paid to select any product.

There are a lot of products on the market, and most parents are confused at the offerings and simply don't know which ones are effective or not. As a result, they rely on independent analysis, reviews, articles, and recommendations from friends. Many articles recommend a number of products for a particular category, like keystroke loggers. The following products are my recommended picks and what I consider to be best of breed in their respective categories.

- Content filtering/monitoring recommendation = CyberPatrol
- Stealth monitoring/keystroke logging recommendation = PC Tattletale

CyberPatrol

CyberPatrol is one of the easiest products to use and is very effective at blocking inappropriate content. It also blocks undesirable services and tools like IM and chat. The product is developed and distributed by Surf Control and is sold via a subscription model for approximately $40 for a one-year subscription and $60 for a two-year subscription. You can purchase the product online at www.cyberpatrol.com. Once purchased and downloaded, simply enter an appropriate license key. The product can be configured for automatic or manual updates. I recommend automatic daily updates that start 10 minutes after your Internet access for that day is initiated. This should be the default setting, so no need to worry about this setting unless you desire less frequent updates. In addition to being an effective tool, CyberPatrol has the following helpful features,

1. Parents can set up individual user profiles for different family members with different filtering permissions. The program has a default user profile that applies to any user on that computer. To simplify configuration, opt for this setting instead of creating multiple user profiles on each computer. You can override any blocks with an administrative password if need be.
2. The product comes with preconfigured filters that are already set up for different age categories. Simply select the filter setting that best applies for the members of your family and it does the rest, which includes automatically setting up permissions for minimum to maximum blocking by information category. Examples of preset filters include Allow All, Adult—Security, Mature Teen, Young Teen, Child, and Custom. I opted for a Custom setting and then went into each of the information categories and set them for the desired filter strength (see Figure 5.1).
3. The product comes with 13 different information categories to allow setting filters at a more detailed level. Categories include Adult/Sexually Explicit, Chat, Criminal Activity & Phishing, Drugs, Alcohol & Tobacco, Gambling, Glamour & Intimate Apparel, Hacking & Spyware, Hate Speech, Remote Proxies, Sex Education, Violence, and Weapons. Figures 5.2 and 5.3 provide screen shots of the various filter options, access levels (on/off, allow, block), and custom settings for each filter option.
4. The product also allows parents to set permissions on a variety of tools

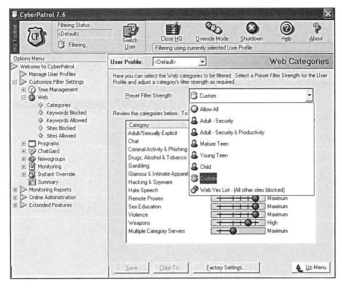

Figure 5.1 Setting Custom Filters
Used with permission from SurfControl PLC.

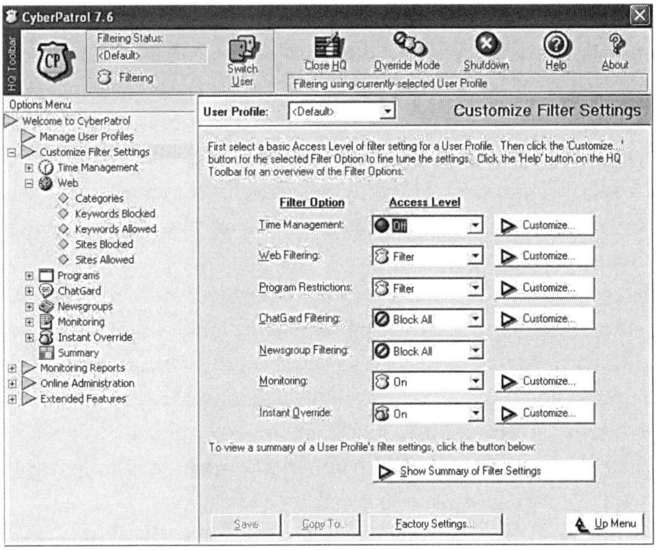

Figure 5.2 Customizing Filter Settings
Used with permission from SurfControl PLC.

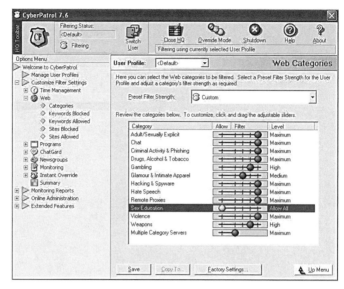

Figure 5.3 Web Categories
Used with permission from SurfControl PLC.

along with blocking them or allowing them individually. An example would be to turn on Web Filtering and customize it while blocking all ChatGard and Usegroups.

5. CyberPatrol allows you to set time restrictions by user account. Parents can allow certain programs to be used only at specific times of the day for each user, if necessary. This may be a helpful feature for working parents whose children may return from school before their parents with a couple of hours to kill on the Internet.

6. The program comes with an instant override feature that allows parents to enter the administrative password for the application and bypass blocks and restrictions that have been set up. I use this feature on all of my home computers and use it to get past blocks that are intended for my children.

7. For Internet Web filtering, the program allows parents to set up blocked and allowed keywords and Web sites that can automatically trigger blocking a Web page from being viewed.

8. Last but not least, the program has a great reporting feature that shows pretty much what was attempted and blocked if monitoring is enabled. I recommend that parents enable this feature at all times.

When a user attempts to access a Web page or Internet service that is blocked, CyberPatrol displays a blocked page/service message prominently for the user. Thus, this product is an overt package for effective Internet monitoring and filtering. For the price, functionality, and automatic updates, CyberPatrol is a must-have for parents with children between the ages of 8 to 17. Unlike individual browser-specific content filters, CyberPatrol works across all browsers with up-to-date licenses. It even protects and logs activities by teenagers trying to access the Internet using a different service provider with their laptop and CyberPatrol installed.

PC Tattletale

PC Tattletale is one of the most unique and effective software programs I've come across in a long time. As a former software developer, I appreciate a good product that doesn't take a whole lot of computing resources and can be set to be completely hidden from the user. Teenagers won't even know that it's installed because the program doesn't show up in the Task Manager as an application, hides all shortcut icons, doesn't show on the program listings, and isn't seen as an installed program from the Control Panel. In addition, the application was engineered to take about as much memory and computer processing power as a small IM program. Thus, it's got a small footprint and can't be seen once it's been installed. Parents can access the management screen by either typing a Ctrl-Alt-function key combination followed by an administrative password or by entering a four letter command in a command prompt window, followed by the correct administrative password. The PC Tattletale product has the following helpful features.

1. The product comes with an effective keystroke logger that traps all passwords for any program or Web-based form. This is extremely helpful for parents who want to login as their child and see personal profile pages posted on their children's favorite social networking sites or sift through emails sent and received on that special account that their children may have hidden from their parents.
2. PC Tattletale records all Web site activity and clearly displays what sites were visited by looking into the Web Sites Recorded section from the main menu (see Figure 5.7).
3. The program can be put into a stealth mode, making it invisible to most users. Access to the management console can only occur if the correct

command and password are entered from a DOS-like command window. Refer to the user's manual for this critical information.

4. The best function of this software is its ability to take a picture of the screen every few seconds, store it in a hidden location, and allow you to play it back like a movie when desired (see Figure 5.4). PC Tattletale's Screen Captures section shows all activity performed on the computer, including any attempts to delete online history, cache, messages, move pictures to and from data keys, and so on. It can be configured to take a snapshot every few seconds. The default is four seconds, but you can set it to, say, eight seconds to save space on the hard drive. This feature is well worth the price of this package. The package automatically deletes screen captures older than 30 days in an effort to prevent filling up the hard drive. Once a screen capture movie is viewed, parents can easily delete the logs by clicking on the appropriate icon on the left side of the management console page. This stealth package is a parent's dream and puts you back in control so that you can be more effective at protecting children while on they're on the Internet.

The following steps will help anyone who wants to know more about what their children are doing online get up and running quickly.

1. Download and install the program, then enter the master password that is required to manage the application and settings.

2. Select the Options button at the bottom of the main menu page (see Figure 5.5).

3. Check (a) Record all Website activity, (b) Record screen shots every 8 seconds, (c) Record all keystrokes, (d) Record all windows opened, and (e) Turn off Ctrl-Alt-F5 hot key (see Figure 5.6). Turning off the hot key will prevent teenagers from detecting that the software is even running. To access the management console with this control key sequence turned

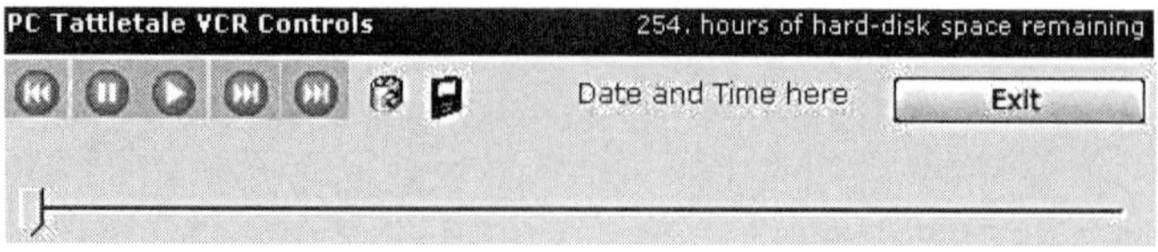

Figure 5.4 PC Tattletale VCR Controls
Used with permission by Parental Controls Products, LLC.

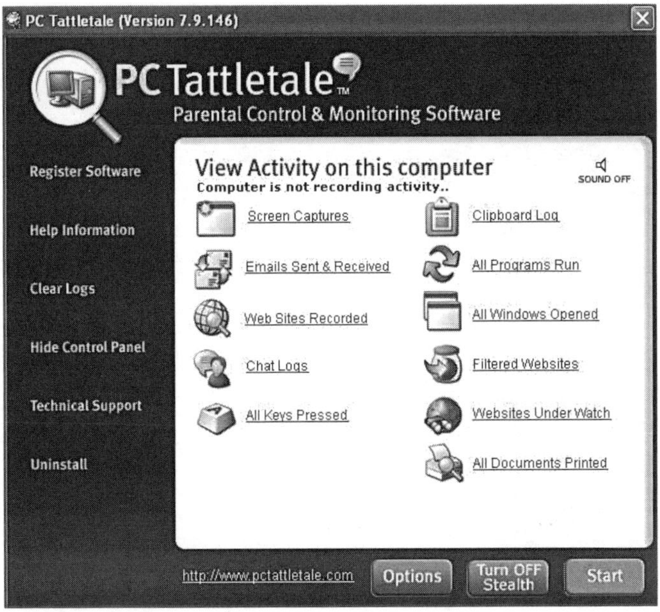

Figure 5.5 PC Tattletale main menu
Used with permission by Parental Controls Products, LLC.

off, please refer to the user's manual for the command to be entered at the command prompt.

4. From the PC Tattletale main menu, turn on stealth monitoring by selecting the Turn ON Stealth button on the bottom of the page.

5. Optional: from the PC Tattletale option menu, select the Scheduling icon on the left to configure the package to turn stealth monitoring on and off at certain times.

6. Optional: from the PC Tattletale option menu, select the ReflexMail icon to be notified via email if certain Web watch keywords are used (say, xxx, sex, etc.) during hours of monitoring.

7. Save your settings.

RECOMMENDATIONS

Parents and teachers who want to monitor children and their online activity need to augment nontechnical monitoring and get up to speed on best practice software solutions like the ones listed in this chapter. Content filtering and

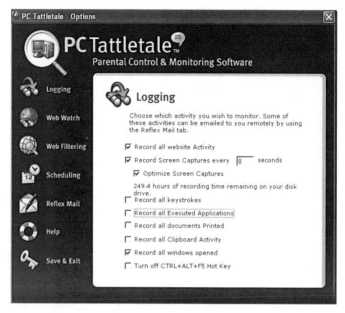

Figure 5.6 PC Tattletale Logging Options
Used with permission by Parental Controls Products, LLC.

monitoring software has come a long way in the past few years and is getting more powerful with every new release. That said, it's by no means perfect and should not be the only technical solution that adults rely on to ensure that their kids are doing the right things and are not putting themselves at risk by posting personal information or conversing with strangers in cyberspace. That's where stealth software like PC Tattletale comes into play. It removes any doubt about what your children are doing on the Internet by providing the clear facts of

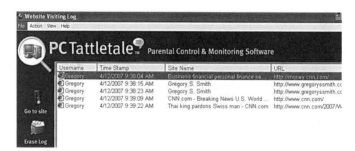

Figure 5.7
Used with permission by Parental Controls Products, LLC.

their online habits, tools, and even with whom they are conversing, regardless of the tool used. Stealth software also fills in the gaps that imperfect content filtering solutions have in the marketplace.

The following recommendations should help parents and teachers get started with great technical solutions that can help keep children safe online. I've also provided recommendations by age category, because from this point on, recommendations will vary by age.

- Avoid external service offerings that are tied to a single Internet service provider. They may be fine as long as your child is younger, but as soon as they get into high school and have access to more mobile types of technology like laptops, PDAs, and so on, these services become less effective as most teens break away from standalone solutions.
- Browser-based content filters like those in Internet Explorer are not effective and are tied to a single browser. Move away from these types of content filtering solutions and install tier-one content filtering software like CyberPatrol. Configure them to update daily and remember to install the software on each PC that is connected to the Internet.
- For the real skinny on what your kids are doing, install the PC Tattletale stealth software on your home computer before installing any content filtering and monitoring software that is overt. Overt software tips children off that they're being monitored. Covert or stealth software reveals what they're really doing. If you find that their activities are less than desired or they are at risk, then by all means install CyberPatrol to better protect them and leave the stealth software up and running to appropriately track their activities, including IM chats, file transfers, and other attempts to cover their online tracks.

Category 1: Elementary School (Ages 8–11)

- The only strong recommendation for this age group is to put Internet filtering software on all computers that children use to access the Internet. My recommendation is CyberPatrol.
- Internet filtering settings should be strong and tied to their age to prevent access to inappropriate content, which is usually by accident. I recommend blocking the following categories for this age group: social networking sites, file sharing/peer-to-peer services, email, FTP, adult content, IM tools, and chat rooms. CyberPatrol makes it easy to apply these settings by selecting the appropriate age profile.

Category 2: Middle School (Ages 12–14)

- Children aged 12–14 are usually going through a transition from child to teenager, which includes all of the wonderful and sometimes interesting mood swings that go along with puberty. All children at this group should have all Internet filtering software installed on all of the computers they use to access the Internet.
- I recommend blocking the following categories for this age group: social networking sites, file sharing/peer-to-peer services, IM tools, FTP, adult content, and chat rooms. CyberPatrol has easy-to-use settings that accomplish this by selecting the appropriate age profile.
- If you decide to allow certain more mature categories like social networking or IM, I highly recommend installing PC Tattletale to capture passwords and monitor their activities so that you can see what they're really doing online. Actions required by parents may include logging into their children's email and social networking accounts to see what they've sent, received, and posted to private audiences vs. the public Internet.
- Change administrative passwords for your Internet filtering and stealth software from time to time, perhaps monthly, as teens at this age may attempt to bypass these controls.

Category 3: High School (Ages 15–17)

- Children aged 15–17 are evolving into young adults, which will probably require allowing more online liberties and freedom. Children in this group should have Internet filtering software like CyberPatrol installed on all of the computers that they use to access the Internet, especially those with wireless network cards.
- Internet filtering settings should be more permissible and tied to their age to prevent access to inappropriate content. I recommend blocking the following categories for this age group: adult content, FTP, file sharing/peer-to-peer services, and chat rooms.
- For this age group, I highly recommend installing PC Tattletale to capture passwords and monitor activities so that you can see what they're really doing online. Teens often use laptop PCs and other Internet providers, some wireless. Stealth software will capture exactly what they're doing online, regardless of where they take their laptop. Parents should review logs weekly and delete as appropriate to free up space as needed for future stealth logs.
- Change administrative passwords for your Internet filtering and stealth software from time to time, perhaps monthly, as teens at this age may attempt to bypass these controls.

Internet Surfing, Blogs, and Social Networking

You're two clicks away from just about anything.

—Gregory S. Smith

SURFING/BROWSING THE INTERNET

It's official—we crossed the 100 million mark for the number of Web sites on the Internet.[1] According to Netcraft, an Internet monitoring company based in Bath, England, the milestone was reached sometime in October 2006.[2] "There are now 100 million web sites with domain names and content on them," according to Rich Miller.[3] That doesn't include all of the sub-domain and personal Web sites on the Net, which are typically not registered and take up only a few pages. The growth in the number of Web sites and content therein is simply staggering and has grown from approximately 18,000 thousand Web sites in 1995.[4] What's more interesting is the rate at which content and number of sites is increasing on the Internet. According to a Microsoft advertisement for their search engine, Live.com, "7 million new pages are added to the Internet every day."[5]

SEARCH ENGINES: THE GOOD, THE BAD, AND THE UGLY

Surfing the Internet today is a crapshoot with regard to what people can find and how easily. The quote at the beginning of this chapter is really true. A well-structured set of keywords with the appropriate Boolean logic (and, or, not, etc.) usually returns relevant links to desired content in a matter of seconds. That content could be anything—schoolwork related, history, computers, travel, pornography photos and movies, S&M, violence, mutilation, racism, guts and gore, gay and lesbian, suicide, eating disorders, drugs, and weapons—all of which can be found with just two clicks of a computer mouse, one to execute the desired search and the second to view the resulting link. From Chapter 3, we know that search engines are great at finding information on the Internet, fast, and yes, dangerous if children are left to use them without proper supervision or filtering software. A recent report conducted by the Harvard Law School's Berkman Center for Internet and Society criticized Google's adult content filter for blocking nonporn sites (such as the American Library Association) when Google's Safe Search is turned on, pointing out that its filters are not 100 percent effective.[6] What does that mean about how accurate their algorithms are for blocking inappropriate content? These algorithms are not that accurate.

The most popular search sites are usually marketed well by the owning company or via social networking. Adults and teens alike seem to gravitate to public search engines that have the lion's share of Internet traffic. The following list includes some popular search sites along with the percentage of searches handled as of July 2006 according to a review of 57 search sites by Hitwise.[7]

- Google (www.google.com): 60.2 percent
- Yahoo! (search.yahoo.com): 22.5 percent
- MSN (search.msn.com): 11.8 percent
- Ask (www.ask.com): 3.3 percent
- AOL (search.aol.com): 1.0 percent
- Others: 1.0 percent collectively

Most of the search tools on the market offer parental or safe search filters, but according to my own research and testing, they don't work as well as I would like, and I don't recommend them for protecting children from potentially harmful content. Not all search sites are the same. My testing reports that Google and Live contain the most content when comparing search phrases and results across the various search engines. Search engine size is usually determined by one statistic—the number of documents indexed or ready for search. Over the past few years, a number of search engines have claimed to be the biggest. In 1997, Altavista claimed the largest repository with nearly 150 million pages indexed.[8] By 2003, the biggest site battle was between AlltheWeb and Google.com with 3.3 billion and 3.2 billion, respectively.[9] Toward the end of 2004, Google had taken over the lead again with 8 billion pages compared to its next rival, MSN, with 4 billion.[10] Today, success of a search engine is determined by a number of factors, including size, speed, marketing, the coolness factor, and growth potential (usually driven by advertising revenue). Google is at the top of that list, but Microsoft is back in the hunt with Live.com.

Search engines can search not only Web pages or HTML documents but within more than 250 file types including some popular files like Word, Power Point, Excel, PDF, WordPerfect, CorelDraw, and even relational databases from vendors like Oracle and IBM. Search engines update their content by sending search robots to look for new and updated content by spidering through pages and links to follow other pages and then updating their directory of indexed content. Many search engines also license their technology for purchase so that companies and organizations can implement sub-search site capabilities on their own corporate, government, and organization-wide public Web sites. Google is one such company that sells hardware appliances loaded with their search tool for groups to use internally on intranets as well as for external public Web sites. As a result, we surf the Web in an environment of organizational search sites specific to each company's content or message, along with a vast repository of external public free search sites with billions of pages of indexed and searchable content. That's really cool, but it comes with a cost. Let me be really clear as I lead into the next section—public free search sites are dangerous for children and should be greatly restricted and limited. It's that simple. I block them for my children using CyberPatrol.

Fortunately, there are a variety of options for parents today. The following sites are good alternatives and can be added (if necessary) to your approved site list in CyberPatrol.

- www.ajkids.com (Ask Jeeves for kids)
- www.kidsclick.org (Web search for kids by librarians)
- www.yahooligans.com (Yahoo! for kids)

Ask Jeeves for kids is one of my favorites because it supposedly contains no content on CyberPatrol's master block list, which is updated frequently.[11] I also like Yahooligans, which is designed for children between the ages of 7 and 12 and contains no adult-oriented advertisements.[12] Other lesser known safe sites include the following.

- www.ala.org/greatsites (American Library Association safe sites for kids)
- www.awesomelibrary.org (32,000 carefully reviewed Web sites for kids)
- www.education-world.com

- www.factmonster.com (a kid-friendly online dictionary, encyclopedia, and almanac)
- www.family-source.com (a family-friendly search engine across 1 million pages)
- www.kids.gov (a U.S. government–sponsored site with content by category and links to other safe sites)

Because it's so easy to search for and find hard-core pornography on the Internet, I wanted to spend a bit of time talking about the risks of exposing children to this material. According to Dr. Mary Anne Layden, co-director of the Sexual Trauma and Psychopathology Program, Center for Cognitive Therapy at the University of Pennsylvania, exposing adults and children to pornography can damage an individual's beliefs and behaviors.[13] In her testimony to the U.S. Senate Committee on Commerce, Science and Transportation, she described some additional harms of pornography.

1. Viewing pornography increases the possibility of sexual addiction for the viewer.
2. Clinical research supports that sex addicts are 40 percent likely to lose their spouse; 58 percent are likely to have a negative impact on their finances; and 27–40 percent may lose their jobs.[14]

The impact on children is just as bad, but in a different way that includes the following.

1. They may develop ideas that the images and videos they see are normal and can apply to them.
2. It may increase the likelihood that children will engage in the sexual behaviors that they see.
3. It may increase the likelihood of sexual exposure at an earlier age, thus increasing the risk of pregnancy and sexually transmitted diseases.[15]

A report from Australia stated that children who eventually became sexual predators all had access and experienced pornography on the Internet.[16] In her testimony, Layden also indicated that "there are no studies and no data that indicate a benefit from pornography use."[17] The following teen testimonials regarding their experience with pornography helps substantiate some of the risks.

- Bill (started viewing at 12 years old): "It led me to having sexual intercourse at age 13, trying to do what I saw on the Internet. I got into drugs and wound up at House of Hope."[18]

- Troy says "cyber-porn skewed his view of women. A guy starts treating a girl like a ho. They're just a piece of meat."[19]

One study of 932 sex addicts revealed that 90 percent of men and 77 percent of women who took part in the study indicated that pornography significantly contributed to their addiction.[20]

As I close out this section, there are four main takeaways:

1. Don't rely on search engine safe search settings—they don't work well by themselves.
2. Block popular search engines for younger children through middle school.
3. If you allow mainstream search sites like Google and Live, use adult filter settings within CyberPatrol to block and limit potentially harmful content. CyberPatrol is very effective at blocking harmful text and visual content.
4. Exposure of pornography to children, especially teenagers, can damage their view of what is a normal sexual relationship and lead to inappropriate and demeaning behavior later in life.

SOCIAL NETWORKING AND BLOGGING

I wrote this portion of the book on Santa Cruz Island in the Galápagos, where I expected technology and access to the Internet to be more of a pipe dream than a reality. Not so. Wireless Internet access and Internet cafés are vibrant on the island, and Internet access is available at most hotels via broadband connections. One traveler described the house where she was staying on a recent boat trip to do some snorkeling on the island of Bartolome. She described her friend's house on Santa Cruz as clean with basic amenities, no air conditioning and no hot water, but fully equipped with high-speed wireless Internet access, two computers, and an iPod. I also spoke to a few teenagers who live on Santa Cruz and they seemed quite aware of the types of content available on the Internet. Several of them indicated that they had free email accounts. I don't know how many teens on the island are aware of or use social networking sites, but it's just a matter of time before this becomes common even in remote locations. Technology is permeating most cultures and locations around the globe, which means that the risks to children on the Internet are just as real on remote islands as they are anywhere else, if not more so.

Social networking and supporting Web sites present real challenges for parents, teachers, and children. Popular sites such as MySpace, Xanga, and Friendster are drawing millions of teens and adults in what appears to be a race for the largest online diary of members. Although hip for kids, who often post pictures of themselves and friends, describe their personal interests, and blog (the act of writing an online diary, a Web log) about daily life, these sites are a parent's worst online nightmare. Kids frequently post too much personal information about themselves, and some operators of these sites have security issues and don't have sufficient mechanisms to protect private profile content for their members. On September 7, 2006, Xanga agreed to pay a $1 million fine for violations of the Children's Online Privacy Protection Act (COPPA) for allegedly collecting and disclosing personal information from kids 12 years old and under.[21] COPPA requires that all commercial Web sites obtain consent from parents before collecting personal information from kids younger than age 13.

What's interesting is what drives average people to blog on the Internet and potentially disclose personal information to millions of strangers. The Internet and social networking sites have helped create a new class of personal reporters and commentators that are eager and willing to write just about anything. A national survey reveals that most bloggers focus on describing their daily life and personal experiences targeted to a small audience; and that only a small percentage of bloggers target their information for larger audiences that include subject areas on politics, media, and government.[22] Although blogging is wildly popular with teens, they're not the only ones writing about their experiences. According to the Pew Research Center, the number of adult bloggers in the United States is on the rise as well—to approximately 12 million adults or 8 percent of adult Internet users.[23] The Pew study goes on to report the following summary findings.

- 54 percent of bloggers say they've never published before anywhere else.
- 54 percent of bloggers are under the age of 30.
- Women and men are almost evenly split among the blogging population.
- 76 percent of bloggers share their personal experiences.[24]

So how big is the social networking market? The answer is simple—it's huge! Table 6.1 offers a slice of data about the larger sites, plus a few alternatives that most parents have not yet heard of by name, along with the number of visitors in 2006 and growth rates from 2005.

Other lesser known sites include XuQa and Hi5, which offer nontraditional add-on services like games and music players.[26] Some kids spend several hours a day on social networking sites, keeping in touch with friends, uploading pictures, and writing in their online journal. As kids have learned that parents are

Table 6.1 Social Networking Sites

Site	2006 Visitors	Percent Change from 2005
MySpace	79.6 million	+243%
Facebook	15.5 million	+86%
Friendster	15.4 million	−1%
LiveJournal	11.6 million	+4%
Piczo	10.2 million	+216%
Bebo	9 million	+185%

Source: comScore World Metrix.[25]

aware of sites like MySpace, they sometimes move to lesser known sites like Piczo to fly under the parental radar. Some sites are more focused on younger teens, whereas others (like Facebook) target older teens to college students. Facebook started out requiring college domain email addresses (like .edu) to register but later opened their site to include high school students.[27]

Although it may be fun for kids and college students to converse online and post personal journals, social networking sites are prime lurking spots for sexual predators. According to a *Washington Post* article, a MySpace member discovered that a stranger had copied her photos from the site, set up a fake page, posted copies of those photos on the new site, and used it to start a relationship with a boy on the west coast.[28] How easy is it for a predator to find potential prey that live close by to them? Unfortunately, it's really simple. On MySpace, predators can simply click on the Browse menu item, enter search information into the categories (including sex, age, country), and then enter the desired ZIP code to search for prospective prey. The ZIP code search can even be refined to include a radius surrounding the desired area to hone in to members within, say, 5 or 10 miles.

Predators often pose as minors on social networking sites, including posting fake photos of themselves, to target victims. Using search technology, they can easily find publicly available content, including email addresses, IM screen names, hobbies, favorite chat rooms, and school names before attempting to establish an online conversation with their next potential victim. "This is the kind of place that clearly attracts sexual predators," states FBI's Child Sexual Victims Agent Jim Clemente.[29] "It's a huge risk," he concludes. How revealing are some of the postings on social networking sites? More revealing than most parents would allow. According to recent RecordOnline.com article, a random search through a dozen or so member profiles in a particular ZIP code revealed a photo of a nearly topless woman who's an admitted dancer, along with a racy bio.[30] A recent search on MySpace resulted in numerous photos, postings, and videos with sexual undertones that are not suitable for children.

Predators also use other tools to hone in on their victims after gaining some ground with key personal facts. Chapter 8 discusses some scary approaches and tools used, including IM and chat rooms, that allow predators to actually locate the address and school within an hour or so of online research. One 14-year old girl is suing MySpace, on which she met a man she alleges sexually assaulted her.[31] The man claims he's not guilty and that the girl, then 13, portrayed herself as 15 years old to get listed on the site, which prohibits users under 14 years old.[32]

Some adults aren't taking the risks of social networking sites lying down. Seven students at a New Jersey high school were suspended for posting photos and profanity on a Web site about other students and teachers.[33] According to school officials, the students used cell phone cameras to secretly take pictures of others without their permission.[34] So, what can parents do about social networking sites? The following quick tips can help.

- Block social networking sites for elementary and middle school children.
- Frequently remind children to never post anything personal that can tip off a sexual predator.
- If access to social networking sites is allowed, stealth monitor via PC Tattletale and review the movie presentations frequently to ensure that your children are not talking to the wrong people online or posting personal content that can be used against them or put them at risk.
- Don't underestimate the appeal of social networking sites for teenagers. They sometimes feel more independent expressing themselves online than in person and don't have to deal with one-on-one embarrassment if they say something wrong.

Don't Forget about FTP Sites

FTP sites are very simple and nongraphical sites for storing and exchanging files among users. Businesses use them to securely send and receive files between vendors and partners. An FTP site uses a different software protocol, denoted by ftp in the Web browser's address line, that is different than the http protocol that is used to access standard Web sites and pages. FTP sites can be accessed with a typical browser in one of two ways:

- anonymous (no user ID/password required), such as ftp://ftp.sitename.com
- user ID/password required, such as ftp://username@ftp.sitename.com; this will likely prompt the user to enter a password

The bad news about FTP sites is:

- Porn (pictures/video) can easily be shared among others who know the FTP address of a particular site.
- FTP sites are popular for sharing illegal music videos, violating copyright, and are also used by hackers to disguise audio files with computer viruses and worms if downloaded, potentially compromising the user's computer and any confidential data on it.
- Many content-filtering packages don't accurately block access to these sites because they often use cryptic file names and no other content.
- Most parents are clueless about FTP sites and how to access them.

The good news is, the FTP protocol itself can be blocked, denying children access to these sites and content.

I recommend that parents block FTP via a firewall application, which is discussed later in this chapter. For parents who are not running a firewall application on their home computer, *you should*. PC Tattletale will easily expose kids using FTP sites to access inappropriate content and which ones they're accessing.

Most adult users have no need to access FTP sites because most content and file downloads are stored on Web servers and not FTP servers. If you do have a need for using FTP, you're probably in the information technology profession and know how to quickly grant and revoke access when needed so that kids are not exposed to the risks of FTP.

VIDEO CAMERAS GONE WILD

Over the past few years, computer-based video cameras have become increasingly popular among teens and adults as a way to humanize communication over the Internet. Two key drivers that have propelled an increase in the use of these devices are the low entry price of cameras and the increase of broadband Internet connections to homes, schools, and businesses. A fully functional video camera attached to a computer retails for about $50 and includes software that is easy to install and use. Lower grade video cameras are also proliferating in today's cell phones, making them viable devices for recording and distributing mini-movies.

The business world has been using computer video cameras for years to add to encrypted and private online meetings that can display slide presentations and real-time video images on the same screen. The technology has become so simple that many professionals use it without assistance from IT pros. I enjoy plugging in a USB camera to my computer and launching an online meeting with a distant colleague. The online meeting software senses the device and automatically opens a window to display live video.

Video cameras and sites that display videos come with significant risk for children today. Several years ago, a creative young woman named Jenny launched a Web site named Jennycam with nothing more than a computer, a camera, and an always-on Internet connection from her bedroom. The camera was left on at all times and displayed to anyone watching her every move and activity, which included sex. The site became wildly popular and famous, with many curious strangers around the world watching to see her next moves. Fast forward to today and we've got several large amateur video sites like YouTube that contain a variety of homemade video clips, many of which are not suitable for children. These sites make it easy for users to upload new content that can be viewed by thousands across the world within minutes. The explosion of online video-sharing Web sites like YouTube, MySpace (who recently added video capabilities), Yahoo!, Google, and even Microsoft has become the latest challenge for parents trying to protect their kids. YouTube is by far the largest and most successful site, with 20 million visitors per month and an average of 50,000 new video uploads per day.[35]

Most video sharing sites require those uploading clips to acknowledge an agreement, usually via checkbox or button, prohibiting content that is obscene, pornographic, or involves nudity. Like most users on the Web, those who upload rarely read the fine print and often upload objectionable content any-way—many knowing that their postings may be removed at a later date. Thus, these objectionable video clips are accessible for a period of time and are only pulled off the site after viewers alert the hosting company about inappropriate content. According to a YouTube spokesperson, "The really objectionable material gets flagged very quickly," and is pulled from the site within 15 minutes.[36] However, not all flagged content is removed from many of these sites, but instead only made available to registered users who are 18 years and older.[37] This approach doesn't help protect children from viewing racy videos. Kids may simply lie about their age when registering; the sites know that this is a common practice, but they have not gone far enough to protect minors. One good way would be to require a credit card to register as 18 and older, but many companies know that they would lose members if they did so. I personally think that management at social networking and video sharing sites are part of the problem and trade child safety for more members and advertising revenue. Shameful!!!

So what are the risks for children using computer-based video cameras and sharing sites? The following summarizes the main risks to children.

- It's easy for children to access inappropriate and mature video content from video-sharing sites.
- These sites, including social networking components, may expose personal information, including what the child looks like or other facts revealed in homemade videos like street names or schools to predators and kidnappers.
- Content including still pictures and video clips can be used by sexual predators to blackmail children into performing other online activities, including sex acts, or even force a face-to-face meeting.

In addition to sometimes entertaining but risky video sharing sites like YouTube, there are thousands of adult sites that have free viewable teaser video clips of people engaging in a variety of sex acts—all accessible without a credit card or being a member of their service. These sites are easily found with a search engine by typing phrases like "sex video."

It is not uncommon for sexual predators to pose as a friend or classmate of a child they've met online. Over the course of days and sometimes weeks of online conversations, predators attempt to build trust and can falsely convince a child that they are really one of their friends at school. In this type of an environment, one thing leads to another and what starts out as, say, a casual topless flash by the child/teenager, turns into a blackmail request (perhaps to post still photos of the flash on the Internet or even mail them to the teen's parents, teachers, and friends). On the extreme side, a misused video camera by a teenager could lead to becoming an online or in-person sex slave to a sexual predator. There are many documented cases that attest to this type of approach and risk.

Parents are thus cautioned to carefully monitor their child's use of video equipment, including cell phones and Webcams. An extreme case of an attempt to block inappropriate video content from children is the recent announcement by a Brazilian telecommunications giant Brazil Telecom SA that they blocked YouTube in part of the country after a steamy sex video of a model and her boyfriend was posted on the site.[38] The widely viewed video became even more notorious after the telecom giant's news to block YouTube made headlines worldwide, but by then the video had been posted to a number of other Web sites, making it almost impossible to block from viewers in Brazil or around the world.[39]

Parents should limit the use of computer-attached video cameras in the home and block video-sharing sites. If computer-based video cameras are installed and used at home, pay attention to how your kids are using them and what sites they are viewing. If necessary, PC Tattletale will tell all on this one.

FIREWALLS AND WIRELESS

Firewalls

Chapter 2 defined a firewall and briefly discussed why parents and teachers need to know about them. Here I cover how to get started selecting and using them. In short, firewalls help parents by:

1. protecting their computer from hackers,
2. blocking certain types of applications from accessing the Internet (usually through a specific firewall port number),
3. blocking certain harmful file types (MP3, EXE, PIF) from being sent by your computer or received by another), and
4. blocking certain protocols (like FTP) from your computer.

This book is not designed to teach parents the ins and outs of firewall technology. Instead I cover just the portions that can help protect children on the Web (e.g., blocking FTP services), so I'll focus on the last benefit. Recommendation: Each computer in your house should have a firewall program installed and running if the computer is connected to the Internet. While most businesses run on expensive hardware/software combined firewalls to protect their computers, consumers typically run free software-only firewalls. Windows XP and Vista come with software firewalls pre-installed. Although these are not as effective as other firewall products, they can be a good first line of defense and are easy to activate with as little as a checkbox. I turn on the firewall for each computer in my home. To activate the Microsoft firewall, simply consult the built-in help program (F1 key) and follow the easy instructions.

Recommendation: Although there are several good software firewall products on the market, I specifically recommend one of the following two.

1. BlackICE PC Protection from Internet Security Systems (ISS), www. BlackICE.iss.net. This program retails for a one-time cost of about $40, but it can be purchased for multiple computers (up to three) for about $100.

2. F-Secure Internet Security 2007, www.f-secure.com. License for one to three computers is approximately $80)

After you've selected a program and downloaded and installed it, please consult the product's online help on how to specifically block FTP as a service. This may require you to block a specific port number, possibly port 21, which is commonly used by FTP. Once blocked, try to access a site like ftp://ftp.micro soft.com and see if the request is stopped by your new firewall rule. If so, congratulations! You've just created a security role in your firewall product.

Wireless

Wireless (Wi-Fi) computing is becoming more the norm these days than the exception. Companies and individuals alike are using wireless access points and networking cards from vendors like Linksys and D-Link to create fast, inexpensive wireless networks, where all connected computers are capable of accessing the Internet. It's certainly cheaper to set up a Wi-Fi network at home than pay to have each room wired with networking cables. Wireless is here to stay, and it presents additional challenges to adequately protect children on the Internet. Today's caregivers and teachers *must* get up to speed on how best to monitor and protect children in a wireless world. The following outlines some of the risks of wireless networking and children using a desktop, but mainly laptop computers equipped with wireless cards (often called wireless NICs).

- Mobile computers with wireless access can bypass Internet security service protections by simply connecting to another unsecured wireless access point to access the Internet.
- Laptops can be used in places where parents can't easily monitor them. PC Tattletale should be installed on them to accurately report what they're being used for, regardless of where they are connected.
- Laptops can bypass home hardware firewalls (sometimes called firewall appliances) by accessing the Internet through another Wi-Fi access point. I recommend installing software firewalls on the computer itself, and then blocking children from uninstalling them with a user account with full operating system administrator privileges.
- Instead of spending the next several pages talking about wireless networks and security, I offer the following simple advice.

1. Install CyberPatrol and set blocks for appropriate ages on any laptop used by a child.
2. If Wi-Fi is enabled, install PC Tattletale with stealth and review usage frequently.
3. If unacceptable violations occur, warn once, then revoke the laptop and give them use of a desktop PC with or without Internet depending on the severity of inappropriate use.
4. Laptops should be considered a luxury item for your children, and they need to know that if the privilege is misused, there will be repercussions, including revoking Internet access or the laptop itself.

RECOMMENDATIONS

I know that there's a lot of material to digest in this chapter, but the topics are important for parents and educators to understand. This chapter contains important information to have a solid grasp of, along with Chapter 5, which discusses specific software programs to help monitor and protect children. The following recommendations are provided to help parents get started in this area. Recommendations are broken down by age category.

All Ages

- Use the built-in personal firewall in Windows.
- Use a software firewall program (BlackICE or F-Secure) to better protect incoming and outgoing traffic.
- Lock down children's user accounts on computers in the home to prevent them from installing software. This should work well without any resistance from elementary and middle school children. For Windows XP, open the Control Panel, select User Accounts, select the appropriate user, select Change my account type to limited.
- Install PC Tattletale on all laptops in the home and enable stealth mode from time to time for middle and high school children. Review usage via the play-back feature as needed.
- Using your software firewall, block the FTP protocol for all users.

Category 1: Elementary School (Ages 8–11)

- Enable CyberPatrol Internet filtering software on all computers that children use to access the Internet and set the filter strength to Custom. For this age category, I recommend blocking newsgroups and chatgard.

- Within CyberPatrol, set *all* of the Web categories (adult/sexually explicit, chat, etc.) to the *maximum* strength filter. The easiest way to do this is to select the preset filter strength = Child, which is accessible in the Web categories section.
- Add the following search engines and social networking sites to Cyber Patrol's blocked list:

  - www.google.com
  - www.altavista.com
  - www.ask.com
  - http://search.aol.com
  - http://search.msn.com
  - www.live.com
  - http://search.yahoo.com
  - www.myspace.com
  - www.friendster.com
  - www.xanga.com
  - www.facebook.com
  - www.livejournal.com
  - www.piczo.com
  - www.bebo.com
  - www.xuqa.com
  - www.hi5.com

- If necessary, add the recommended safe search sites listed in this chapter to the CyberPatrol approved site list.

Category 2: Middle School (Ages 12–14)

- Children aged 12–14 are going through an interesting transition from children to teenager. All children in this group should have Internet filtering software installed on all of the computers that they use.
- Within CyberPatrol, set *all* of the Web categories (adult/sexually explicit, chat, etc.) to a *high* or *maximum* strength filter. The easiest way to do this is to select the preset filter strength = Young Teen, which is accessible in the Web categories section.
- Add the following search engines and social networking sites to Cyber Patrol's Web sites blocked list:

  - www.google.com
  - www.altavista.com

- www.ask.com
- http://search.aol.com
- http://search.msn.com
- www.live.com
- http://search.yahoo.com
- www.myspace.com
- www.friendster.com
- www.xanga.com
- www.facebook.com
- www.livejournal.com
- www.piczo.com
- www.bebo.com
- www.xuqa.com
- www.hi5.com

- Read *MySpace Unraveled* by Larry Magid and Anne Collier (available at bookstores and online at Amazon.com). This book is not terribly long, but it serves as a good reference for how the hottest social networking site works along with some helpful tips for parents.
- If you decide to allow certain more mature categories like social networking or IM, I highly recommend installing PC Tattletale and enabling stealth mode so that you can appropriately monitor what they're doing online. Actions required by parents may include logging into their children's social networking accounts to see what they've sent, received, and posted to private audiences versus the public Internet. If you find activities of sites accessed that you don't approve of, simply add those sites to the Cyber Patrol list of blocked sites.
- Change administrative passwords for CyberPatrol, PC Tattletale, and your home computer's operating system from time to time. I recommend monthly to quarterly as teenagers may attempt to bypass these controls by guessing your passwords.
- Using your software firewall, block the FTP protocol for all users.
- Add appropriate keywords to CyberPatrol's blocked keywords list to ensure that kids can't find inappropriate material. Add the following: porn, sex, xxx, gay, lesbian, nude, and naked. Use your imagination and add to this list as you see fit.

Category 3: High School (Ages 15–17)

- Children aged 15–17 are evolving into young adults, which requires allowing more online liberties and freedom. Teenagers should have Internet filtering software installed on all of the computers that they use to access the Internet, especially those with wireless network cards.

- Within CyberPatrol, set *all* of the Web categories (adult/sexually explicit, chat, etc.) to a *medium* through *maximum* strength filter. The easiest way to do this is to select the preset filter strength = Mature Teen, which is accessible in the Web categories section. Keep in mind, using this setting allows chat, so I recommend setting it to a much higher filter strength (say, high)—chat rooms are risky even for mature teens.
- Teenagers will most likely be using full-strength search engines in support of their schoolwork, so you'll need to add to CyberPatrol's approved Web site list:

  - www.google.com
  - www.altavista.com
  - www.ask.com
  - http://search.aol.com
  - http://search.msn.com
  - www.live.com
  - http://search.yahoo.com

- If you decide to allow more mature categories like social networking or IM, install PC Tattletale and enable stealth mode so that you can appropriately monitor what they're doing online. If you find activities on sites accessed that you don't approve of, simply add those sites to the CyberPatrol list of blocked sites. For this age group, PC Tattletale exposes more sophisticated approaches to sharing and concealing inappropriate content. Data keys seem to be the tool of choice for storing files away from the home computer where they can be easily searched by parents. PC Tattletale puts parents back in charge of computer and Internet security for their children. For this age category, it should be used frequently to ensure that kids are safe on the Internet. It will record all activities, including data key file transfers and thus help keep children safe by keeping parents in the loop.
- Change administrative passwords for CyberPatrol, PC Tattletale, and your home computer's operating system from time to time. I recommend monthly to quarterly as teenagers may attempt to bypass these controls by guessing your passwords.
- Maintain a list of blocked keywords in CyberPatrol that are appropriate for your mature teen.

Seven

Email

Email is the electronic leash of the modern day. Instant messaging will replace it in the near future.

—Gregory S. Smith

EMAIL OPTIONS AND PROGRAMS

This chapter will likely be one of the easiest for parents and teachers to understand because many adults in industrialized and developing nations have and actively use an email account. Quite a few working parents have two accounts, one for business and one for personal messages. Most children, starting with middle school and into high school, have multiple email accounts, sometimes as many as five or six. Why? Usually for the following three reasons: (1) It's easy to set up a free account. (2) They do so to assert their independence. (3) They do so to elude monitoring from their parents. If you think you're on top of monitoring your teenager's online mail, you're probably mistaken—they may have multiple free accounts at mail services like Yahoo!, Google, Microsoft, and Lycos. According to About.com, the following are some of the top free email Web sites and services available.

1. Gmail (Google)
2. Inbox.com
3. Yahoo! Mail
4. AIM Mail (AOL)

5. Goowy Mail
6. Hotmail
7. Lycos Mail[1]

Beyond these examples, there are literally hundreds of alternative sites that children can use to sign up for free and use Web-based email programs—many without their parents' knowledge. If this isn't a great reason to stealth monitor your child's email activities, I don't know what is. Parents can't possibly have the time to keep track of the various email accounts and passwords. A far better use of their time is to use PC Tattletale (see Chapter 5) and let the software program do what it does best—record children's online activities.

Types of Email Service

There are essentially three main types of email services.

- Web-based
- POP3
- IMAP[2]

Web-based mail is probably the most common among children, especially teens, because they can access their account from a Web browser and an Internet connection from pretty much anywhere on the planet. All messages, sent, received, and stored in personal folders are maintained online at the mail hosting provider for each user.

POP3 email services initially store email on the hosted server from the email provider. Users select from a variety of robust email packages, like Outlook or Eudora, and install the desired program to have more features. POP3 users usually access their email on the remote POP3 server, download new messages to their computer, and send messages authored and queued to be sent. Users can typically configure a POP3 account to delete messages already downloaded from the hosted server or keep a second copy. Most POP3 users use local email and POP3 services because it's easier and faster to write and read messages on their computer, especially with low-speed Internet connections, compared to waiting for Web pages to refresh in a browser's window. This approach also allows users to manage larger amounts of email and file attachments on their own computer and not have to worry about disk space limitations for most online Web email services, which tend to limit disk space per user to between 50 MB and 2 GB. Email messages with large file attachments can quickly fill up a Web-based email system quota. Like POP3, IMAP works with an email program to download email messages from a remote server. In addition, IMAP allows more control such as synchronizing mail folders between a local computer and a remote IMAP server.

The following are several popular free email programs that can be downloaded and installed on Windows-based computers.

- Mozilla Thunderbird
- Eudora
- Opera
- Outlook Express
- Pegasus Mail[3]

Thunderbird, Opera, and Outlook Express are probably the most popular programs; each has solid third-party reviews and robust features. Your child is probably using either a Web-based service or accessing email through one of these programs.

EMAIL RISKS

So what are the risks of children using email today? The following are what I consider to be the top five threats.

1. Predators look for email addresses on Web sites and social networking sites, then expand their search for more relevant and personal information.
2. Spam (unwanted email) can reach children with a variety of tricks (scams) or inappropriate content, such as graphic pornography or seemingly harmless links that actually go to adult content sites.
3. Computer viruses and worms can damage a computer, increase the risk of information loss, and require expensive consulting to repair. Kids typically open more file attachments or messages from strangers than adults. Some of these files contain harmful computer viruses. Special offer scams typically try to trick teens into giving up personal information to obtain a fake prize, like winning an iPod.
4. Many children using email software disclose their full name every time they send an email. This is often referred to as a "user name," "full name," or "real name" in email programs like Outlook Express. Send yourself an email from your child's installed email program and see if their full name appears in the From heading. If it does, it should be changed in the

program to only disclose, say, a first name or an irrelevant alias, which is even safer. Consult your specific email program's help section for instructions on how to change the sent user name.

5. Some free Web mail isn't secure, which is usually indicated by the lack of a locked key logo on the browser's window. User IDs and passwords can be compromised by hackers and predators, because the text for the account and password pass across the Internet unencrypted.

KID-FRIENDLY EMAIL PROGRAMS

Fortunately, there are a number of kid-friendly email programs available, most for a small monthly fee. Several are fairly good at greatly reducing spam and eliminating porn from arriving in your child's inbox. Of course, no one can guarantee a risk-free email experience, especially if your child posts his or her email address on a public Web page or social networking site or trades inappropriate files and photos. The following services are some great alternatives to risky free email services for children and teenagers.

- Kidmail.net (currently $6 per month after a free trial or $30 per year for up to 10 email addresses; www.kidmail.net)
- Zoobuh.com (30-day free trial, then $1 per month per child account; www.zoobuh.com)
- AOL email with AOL Parental Controls enabled (site.aol.com/info/parent control.adp)
- Earthlink with Parental Controls enabled (earthlink.net/software/free/parentalcontrols)

The first two are typically geared toward parents with younger children (elementary to the beginning of middle school) and have lots of parental controls, such as determining who can email the child's account, parental review/approval of unknown incoming mail before it gets to a child's inbox, and redundant copies of sent and received emails sent to a parent or guardian's email address as kind of an audit trail. Other more mature offerings from Earthlink and AOL (with parental controls enabled) are more suitable for older middle school to high school teenagers and don't come with an adolescent email domain name. Many children use these services but don't enable parental controls. They're missing a valuable option in the arsenal to protect their children. These services without parental controls are too risky even for middle school kids. Offerings like AOL email with parental controls is even configurable for different age ranges, such as young teen (ages 13–15) and mature teen (ages 16–17), that are similar to what CyberPatrol has to offer to ease configuration for Internet content filtering.

TRICKS KIDS USE TO HIDE EMAIL ACTIVITIES

If parents want to be one step ahead of their kids, they need to be tech-savvy and think creatively, like cunning children often do. Kids (mainly teenagers) use the following activities to hide or conceal what they do on email.

- Maintain multiple accounts, often Web-based services, and rotate through them as needed.
- Delete messages from their sent folder and inbox that they don't want their parents to see.
- Send questionable file attachments with innocuous file names, such as homework1.doc or class-notes.xls.
- Save questionable file attachments to data keys or thumb drives to conceal their contents.
- Delete temporary Internet files and history from their browser and hard drive to conceal what they've seen via the Web.

I applaud creativity, but it's no match for PC Tattletale, which records all activity and allows parents to play back hidden recorded files like they're watching a movie (see Chapter 5). That's why I recommend using stealth software for troubled or vulnerable middle school children and all high school teens who are active on the Internet.

BLOCKING FREE EMAIL SERVICES

This part is simple. To block free email services that are risky, such as the ones listed earlier in the chapter, simply add the Web sites to the CyberPatrol blocked sites list and voilà! You're done! If you think your child is using another version of an email program, you can do the following.

- Install PC Tattletale and enable it in stealth mode.
- Capture Web site activities, including account names and passwords.
- Log into their new email accounts and take a look for suspicious or inappropriate email.
- If desired, add the new email site/service to the CyberPatrol blocked list.

Some Web sites/services make it harder for minors to open a new account than others. Security-conscious sites not only ask for age verification but also require a credit card to activate a free account in an attempt to protect minors. Unfortunately, it's still relatively easy for a child to find a free email service and sign up without any parental involvement or approval. Within about three minutes, I was able to successfully set up Web-based email accounts on both Yahoo! mail and Mail.com by simply lying about my age, selecting an email address name, and accepting the terms displayed on the site—all without any parental approval or requirement for a credit card. The recommendations section at the end of this chapter contains specific free email Web site addresses that parents can block to help protect their children. This list is not all-inclusive, but PC Tattletale will expose any others that children are using and can be shut down and blocked by CyberPatrol. Thus, part of the strategy of this book is to arm parents with the right technology and an effective road map to protect their children. PC Tattletale combined with CyberPatrol is the one-two punch that can do the job.

FILE ATTACHMENT RISK

Given that most parents use email and are aware of the risks associated with file attachments, this section will be short and sweet. Talk to your children about the risks (viruses, inappropriate content, predators, etc.) and repeatedly tell them *not* to open attachments or email from anyone they don't know. If you see your children using data keys frequently, they may be storing traded file attachments to avoid inspection by a parent. Ask to see their data keys from time to time and do a file inventory using your computer. Turning on thumbnails for images will allow parents to quickly view image pictures without having to open them one by one. To find out any other file attachment concealment strategies, it's PC Tattletale to the rescue!

DON'T FORGET ABOUT SPAM

Spam is unwanted email. It comes in a variety of forms that can be risky for children, including adult content, inappropriate advertisements, special offers and scams, racially insensitive content, and get-rich-quick schemes. Children who see an offer to receive a free iPod will be more likely click on the link because they truly believe, especially at younger ages, that they've just won a free prize. The reality is that they could be directed to a site that may attempt to capture personal data or, even worse, relay the user to an adult site that displays graphic content, including video clips or still pictures. According to Postini , a world leader in anti-SPAM and anti-virus products and services, spam represents a significant portion of email and is a threat to businesses and consumers.[4] The Postini Resource Center, which tracks spam for their customers, recently reported that every 10 out of 12 email messages, or just over 81.5 percent, were tagged as spam and quarantined for their customers in a normal day.[5] On the particular day that I was monitoring the Postini Web site, the number of messages tagged as spam reached 371,541,404 in a 24-hour period, out of 562,866,069 messages scanned.[6] In addition, during that same 24-hour period, 1 in 335 messages was determined to contain a virus.[7] The numbers reported by Postini clearly demonstrate that spam is a problem for email customers worldwide.

To mitigate the risks of spam, parents can choose one of two options. The first is to install an anti-spam program on their computer, configure it, and set up the program to receive updates as necessary. The second option is to select an email provider that incorporates anti-spam and anti-virus capabilities directly into their email service and attempts to block them before the email is delivered to the account. I strongly advocate the latter approach. It's easier for parents and doesn't require any complicated installations and update procedures. The email services listed earlier in this chapter provide decent anti-spam features as part of their offerings. It's a no-brainer that requires less time and energy. Parents already expend enough energy working, raising children, and trying to protect them online. When something comes along that can help them reduce spam and viruses, even for a fee, it is well worth the cost.

RECOMMENDATIONS

The following recommendations are provided to help parents protect their children against the risks of email and related technologies.

Recommendations for All Ages

- Lock down children's user accounts on computers in the home to prevent them from installing new email software on your computer.
- Install PC Tattletale on all laptops in the home and enable stealth mode from time to time for middle and high school children. Review usage via the movie playback feature as needed and remember to delete log files to prevent filling up disk drives.

- Set a family policy that email account passwords are to be known by parents and not changed by children. If they are changed, revoke their account for a month and add the email service/site to the blocked site list in Cyber Patrol. I'm a fan of warning once before fully revoking a privilege. If your child repeatedly changes an email account password, he or she may be trying to conceal what they're doing online. In this scenario, parents have two options: use PC Tattletale to see exactly what the child is using email for and, if necessary, revoke the privilege, or just revoke email as a privilege until they are older and can better respect the rules. Remember—parenting is not a democracy. It's the parent's job to make the best decisions necessary to protect their children and that means establishing some rules with clear repercussions.

Category 1: Elementary School (Ages 8–11)

- Children in this age category should *not* have an email account. When my children were in this age bracket, I held firm on this position, even though they asked repeatedly and threw tantrums when I said no. Don't budge on this. Cell phones are safer alternatives to email accounts at this age in the event that a child needs to stay in touch with a parent or caregiver.
- My recommendation above is strong, and I recognize that there may be exceptions, such as the use of school email accounts to support homework assignments. If you do allow your younger child to have an email account, use one of the kid-friendly email programs or one that is provided by the school itself. If school provided, check to see if spam is being blocked and, if not, raise the issue with the school principal.
- Kid-friendly email accounts alone won't help keep your child safe, so parents will need to monitor what their kids are doing online. Inspect their email accounts by logging in as them once a week and reviewing files sent and received by navigating through folders and their inbox. If possible, set their deleted folder to not purge data for at least seven days. This will allow parents to view what their child has deleted in the course of using the service over the last week.

Category 2: Middle School (Ages 12–14)

- Set a family policy of one email account per child and enforce it. Allowing children to maintain multiple accounts adds risk and can be time-consuming for parents to monitor. A classic trick that kids at this age use is to use an approved email account while their parents are observing and then use another free email *unapproved* account to elude their parents. If you suspect your child is using multiple accounts, turn on PC Tattletale in stealth mode and analyze their usage. As appropriate, add unapproved sites to the CyberPatrol blocked list to clamp down on violators.

- Kid-friendly email accounts alone won't keep your child entirely safe, so parents will need to monitor what they're kids are doing online. Inspect their email accounts by logging in as them once a week and reviewing files sent and received. If possible, set their deleted folder to not purge data for at least seven days. This will allow parents to view what their child has deleted in the course of using the service.

- Have frequent conversations with your children about the risks of opening and responding to emails from senders they don't know. They should *never* respond to an email from someone that they don't know and *never* open a file attachment from unknown senders as well. If they don't respond to email, they can't potentially give out personal data to a stranger.

- Teach your child to *never* knowingly publish or allow his or her email account names to any public Web site, including a school Web site, which can expose risks of sexual predators. If this occurs unknowingly, contact your school's administrator immediately.

- Ensure that the email provider that you select doesn't flood your child's email account with potentially inappropriate spam. If it does, contact your provider and see if they can correct it. If they cannot, switch to another provider that offers a better anti-spam solution that is built into their email offering. Select one of the four safe email sites/services described earlier in this chapter.

- Add the following free email sites to CyberPatrol's blocked list.

  - http://gmail.google.com, www.google.com/accounts/SmsMailSignup1, www.google.com/accounts/ServiceLoginAuth
  - www.inbox.com, www.inbox.com/register/email.aspx
  - www.goowy.com
  - https://login.yahoo.com/config/mail?.intl=us, www.yahoo.com/r/m1, www.yahoo.com/r/m2
  - http://webmail.aol.com, https://new.aol.com
  - http://hotmail.msn.com, http://login.live.com/login.srf?id=2, http://join.msn.com
  - www.mywaymail.com

- http://mail.lycos.com
- www.mail.com

Category 3: High School (Ages 15–17)

- Set a family policy of one email account per child and enforce it. If you suspect your child is using multiple accounts, turn on PC Tattletale in stealth mode and analyze their usage. As appropriate, add unapproved sites to the CyberPatrol blocked list to clamp down on violations.
- Parents need to more aggressively monitor what their kids are doing online via email and other tools at this age. There are two options: (1) inspecting email accounts by logging in as them once a week and reviewing files sent and received by navigating folders and their inbox, or (2) using PC Tattletale in stealth mode and reviewing their activity on a more frequent basis. Teenagers are more likely to use data keys in support of school projects. Look for exchanges of inappropriate files (videos, pictures, etc.) via your child's email account and attempts to save them (possibly by renaming the files) to their data key. PC Tattletale provides some insights into what may be going on, but at the end of the day, parents may need to ask for their child's data key and inspect what's on it. If the key contains significant objectionable material, parents have a lot of options that include revoking accounts and access to the Internet in general via CyberPatrol.
- Have frequent conversations with your teenagers about the risks of opening and responding to emails from senders that they don't know. They should *never* respond to an email from someone that they don't know and *never* open a file attachment from unknown senders as well.
- Teach your teenagers to *never* knowingly publish or allow email account names to be published on any public Web site—including a school Web site, which can expose risks of sexual predators to children. If this occurs unknowingly, contact your school's administrator immediately.
- Ensure that the email provider that you select doesn't flood your child's email account with potentially inappropriate spam. If it does, contact the provider and see if they can correct it. If they cannot, switch to another provider that offers a better anti-spam solution that is built into their email offering.
- Block the same set of free email sites/services that are recommended for category 2. Earthlink and AOL are good options for teenagers when com-

pared to the other younger branded email domains recommended in this chapter.

- Use PC Tattletale as you see fit to monitor what they're doing online via email, especially if your child is using a laptop equipped with a wireless networking card. Many of the free email services on the Internet can't be blocked by a port number because they mostly use the http protocol and port 80 or 443 (secured login) to communicate. Thus, parents should review the PC Tattletale logs and block sites where appropriate.

Instant Messaging and Voice-over-IP

For a list of all the ways technology has failed to improve the quality of life, please press three.

—Alice Kahn

IM BASICS AND TOOLS

Instant messaging (IM) tools are very popular, especially with younger computer users up to and including Generation X adults working in businesses, nonprofits, and academic institutions. People of all ages are starting to embrace IM because it has recently expanded into cell phones and PDAs. IM traffic sent over the Internet is expected to eclipse that of email by 2012. IM is essentially a software program that enables real-time communication between users, usually facilitated by an intermediary company and service like America Online, Microsoft, or Yahoo! Compared to email, which can take longer to deliver messages because they are queued by mail servers and log all outgoing and incoming mail, IM is more like a quick online chat between two or more parties. Due to the near real-time capability, IM is faster than email and for that reason alone has become the tool of choice for an individual that wants to instantly send a message to another person connected to the Internet.

IM has some financial benefits for its users as well. The number one monetary benefit that I hear all the time is that it's cheaper to place a phone call using IM than to make a long-distance call to another country via a traditional phone company. I personally know many businesses and individuals using IM tools to make phone calls to friends and colleagues in other countries in an effort to save money. This capability is often referred to as a voice-over-IP (or VOIP) feature within the IM program itself. Although many IM tools have voice capabilities, the quality of phone calls made over the Internet can vary greatly from crystal clear calls to delayed ones with significant static.

IM tools have evolved over the past few years with additional entrants into the marketplace. The following describes the main features of IM tools.

- Users can chat with one another. Chatting is essentially sending small text messages to one another over the Internet. Chatting requires both parties to be connected to the Internet and available using the same IM tool to communicate.
- You can send files and pictures to one another. Essentially, most IM tools have built-in FTP capabilities, but many of these tools don't necessarily use that protocol to send and receive files, making them harder to block.
- You can make voice phone calls over the Internet. Headphones or speakers are usually required.
- You can send off-line messages to friends and colleagues. A few IM programs allow this. This functionality resembles that of email and can also provide an audit trail of what was sent and received.
- You can use Web cameras to conduct real-time video sessions or send prerecorded video files to other users, which is similar to sending a file attachment.

Most IM users communicate with others online that are also accessing the Internet via an IM service. Users typically maintain a buddy list (an address list of all their IM friends) and can readily see when their friends are online. There are a variety of IM programs available, most of them free, but they usually don't work together. Microsoft's IM tool, Windows Live Messenger, recently announced that their tool would work with Yahoo!'s Messenger. For the most part though, one vendor's IM program doesn't interoperate and send messages to another vendor's tool. As an example, AOL Instant Messenger will not work with Google Talk. The following are some of the more popular free IM programs available with advanced features indicated.

1. Google Talk (www.google.com/talk): voice calls, offline IM.
2. AOL Instant Messenger (www.aim.com): broadcast messages to many, voice calls with AIM Phoneline, logging of messages, offline IM.
3. ICQ (www.icq.com): voice calls.

4. Yahoo! Messenger (messenger.yahoo.com): voice calls, IM chat with Windows Live Messenger, offline IM.
5. MSN Windows Live Messenger (get.live.com): voice calls, IM chat with Yahoo! Messenger, Web camera/video capable.
6. Skype (www.skype.com): voice calls, group chat (up to 100 people), video camera integration.

Beyond these popular sites, there are plenty more alternative programs and related freeware Web sites and tools that offer IM features. Many of the other freeware and shareware sites may come with additional risks, such as exposure to viruses and spyware. A popular IM tool available via a number of sites is Trillian (www.ceruleanstudios.com). It allows users to talk to pretty much any IM program.

The core list of popular programs combined with hundreds of lesser known sites is justification to apply an aggressive block and stealth monitoring approach to IM, especially for children in elementary and middle school. Parents can't possibly have the time to keep track of the various IM tools and passwords. A far better use of their time is to use CyberPatrol's capabilities and turn on PC Tattletale stealth monitoring as needed to combat the risks. Interestingly enough, when I blocked IM chat in CyberPatrol, it was effective at blocking most IM-related Web sites (but not all of them). The following represents the IM sites that I was and was not able to get to and download IM software with CyberPatrol's chat Web category set to the highest level of blocking:

- Allowed: Google, Yahoo!
- Blocked: AOL, Skype, ICQ, MSN

So what are the real risks for children using IM? Parents see other kids using IM and text messaging from their PCs and cell phones all the time, and may assume there must not be any risk associated with these products. The following represent my top threats associated with children using IM tools.

1. IM provides an easy way for strangers to contact children.
2. IM users can receive unwanted messages, like email, that could contain links to adult content and other inappropriate content.
3. If configured inappropriately, IM tools allow anyone on the service to see the user's contact name, or screen name, and message them as they see fit. Many children, when installing these products, don't check off the box that only allows their buddies to contact them, thus exposing their

screen name to the world. There are additional preference settings that may expose an IM screen name if one knows the user's email address. This type of connection is what predators look for.

4. Unlike email, IM conversations between parties are not typically logged or recorded, unless the user specifically does so. This provides for unaudited communication between parties that parents can't review to determine if their children are at risk. Without some type of monitoring tool like PC Tattletale, parents don't know who their children are IMing and what they're talking about. That's a significant risk.

5. IM tools allow children to share photos and send files without a log or trace for parents to review.

6. IM screen names are often disclosed in chat rooms along with other forums. Predators look for IM names and email addresses on Web sites, in chat rooms, and in social networking sites then expand their search for more relevant and personal information in preparation for finding their next online victim.

7. Many IM tools provide for nondocumented or logged voice calls over the Internet to people anywhere in the world. No sane parent would let their child randomly call a stranger from another country using their home phone. IM voice features provide one of the biggest risks to children that predators love to expose. VOIP between computers is a predator's dream and the easiest way for them to communicate via voice in stealth and beyond a parent's control.

IM LINGO PARENTS MUST KNOW

For parents to truly understand what their children are doing on the Internet, they need to get up to speed on the IM lingo that's used. This is necessary so that parents and teachers can decode online communications and shorthand to meaningful text. Children, especially teenagers, often talk in "code" using IM and chat tools to elude their parents and tip off their online buddy that a parent or older sibling is near or monitoring their IM conversation. Table 8.1 provides a list designed to help parents walk the walk and talk the talk.

BLOCKING IM: IT'S NOT EASY

For parents and teachers to understand how to block IM for younger children, they need to know a bit more about how IM works (see Figure 8.1). IM programs need to be installed on any computer where the user wishes to use it.

Table 8.1 IM Lingo Translated

Code	Translation	Code	Translation
2NITE	tonight	P911	parent alert
ADR	address	PAW	parents are watching
AEAP	as early as possible	PIR	parent in room
ALAP	as late as possible	POS	parent over shoulder
ASL	age/sex/location	QT	cutie
BRB	be right back	RN	right now
F2F	face to face	RU	are you?
GYPO	get your pants off	RUMORF	are you male or female?
IWSN	I want sex now	SITD	still in the dark
KFY	kiss for you	SMEM	send me an email
KPC	keeping parents clueless	SMIM	send me an instant message
LMIRL	let's meet in real life	SO	significant other
LOL	laugh out loud	SorG	straight or gay
MOOS	member of opposite sex	TDTM	talk dirty to me
MorF	male or female	TOM	tomorrow
MOTSS	member of the same sex	TS	tough shit
NAZ	name, address, ZIP	TTFN	ta-ta for now
NIFOC	nude in front of computer	WUF	here are you from?
OLL	online love	WYCM	will you call me?
OTP	on the phone	WYRN	what's your real name?

Source: www.netlingo.com

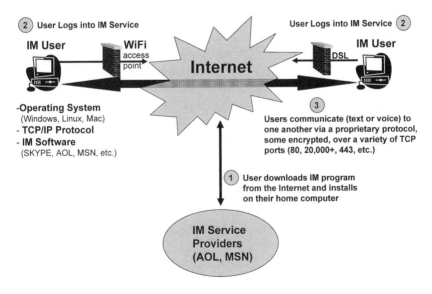

Figure 8.1 How IM Works

The bulk of IM users download their favorite tool from one of the top vendors listed earlier. Once installed, users create a screen name and password that is registered in the IM service provider's directory listing so that other IM users can chat with the new user. Once the registration process is complete, the user can browse from a directory listing of public IM names or simply start building their own buddy list with input from their friends and colleagues. To IM or call someone on the list, users simply double-click the user's screen name and start chatting in real time or send a message to an off-line user.

Most IM products are really hard to block. Many corporations and businesses invest thousands of dollars of time and labor trying to block these tools from their computing environment because they pose security and productivity risks for employers. IM products communicate on various ports, sometimes changing from port to port if a firewall is attempting to block the desired port. There can be literally hundreds of ports that these programs will jump to so as to evade firewalls. Many of the most sophisticated IM products use standard ports that are open for other Web traffic, such as port 80 and port 443, which is used for encrypted traffic. Some IM tools encrypt the communication so that it can't be intercepted across the open Internet and so it can pass through a personal or corporate firewall easily.

Fortunately, there are ways to block IM tools and traffic in the home environment. I've done some extensive testing to confirm that these programs can be effectively blocked. If parents think that just blocking access to the IM Web sites will deter their children from using IM chat clients, they're wrong. Kids are smart. They share downloaded programs with friends and trade installation programs that they can't get access to on the Internet with friends via data keys and CDs. Blocking IM requires the following steps.

1. Block chat in CyberPatrol's tool. Simply set the Web site category chat to maximum block strength and make sure all checkboxes are selected in the ChatGard section under chat programs to monitor.
2. Add additional Web sites listed in the recommendations section of this chapter to block the sites that CyberPatrol doesn't.
3. As needed, use PC Tattletale to monitor and identify other freeware IM tools your children are using and block them in CyberPatrol by using Program Restrictions instead of blocking just the Web site.
4. To close the door on the more difficult IM programs like Skype, parents need to first install the program and then block access to the program itself in CyberPatrol. The following is an example of how to block Skype, but the steps can be applied to any IM tool that you wish to block.

a. Download and install the Skype program.

b. In CyberPatrol, change Program Restrictions access level to Filter instead of Allow All.

c. Select the Customize menu associated with Program Restrictions and then select Customize Programs.

d. Select the Add button, then Find New Programs. I've found that the automatic listing that CyberPatrol doesn't always show all programs installed, which is why I recommend a manual search.

e. Manually locate the Skype program by navigating through the directory structure on the C: or D: drive where the application is installed. To block Skype along with the browser plug-in on the drive, select C:\Program Files\Skype\Phone\Skype and C:\Program Files\Skype\Plug-in Manager\SkypePM.

f. Add both programs to the CyberPatrol program listing.

g. Once added to the list, select each program, one at a time, and click on the access level radio button labeled Deny access at all times.

h. Save your changes for all users or the appropriate user profile.

5. I'd recommend this install and block approach for the Trillian IM tool as well since it's available to download from a lot of Web sites.

The next time a user tries to run Skype, it will be blocked by CyberPatrol and shut down—preventing the user from getting to the Internet using the program entirely. Great stuff!! The combination of the two tools I've recommended in this text (CyberPatrol and PC Tattletale) along with the road map will put parents and educators back in charge of managing their children's Internet experiences.

If parents want to be one step ahead of their kids when they use technology, they need to be tech-savvy and think creatively, like cunning minors often do. Kids, mainly teenagers, use the following activities to hide or conceal what they do on IM.

- Intentionally don't log the conversations, even if the IM tool has the capability.
- Use multiple IM programs.
- Send questionable file attachments with file names intended to not draw attention to them, such as homework1.doc or class-notes.xls.
- Save questionable file attachments to data keys to conceal their contents.

- Delete log files that they have recorded on their computer once the conversation of choice is completed and no longer needed.
- Conduct phone conversations with friends and strangers over the Internet, usually with the aid of a headset.
- Make and send private video clips using IM tools or engage in a real-time video session if the chat client offers that feature.

While I applaud this creativity, it's no match for PC Tattletale, which records all activity and allow parents to play back recorded files, including any of the activities listed above. That's why I recommend using stealth software for challenging middle schoolers and all high school teens that are active on the Internet. Late-night, always-on-the-Internet types of activities are tips for parents that there is something else that may be going on. Homework can't take that long.

CHAT ROOMS: A HANGOUT FOR PREDATORS

Chat rooms, sometimes referred to as online groups, are places for people to discuss just about anything. They are online discussion groups by category where people can login and converse with others. There are thousands of chat rooms on the Internet, hosted by a variety of providers ranging from Yahoo! to MySpace, and of course there are adult chat and video rooms. Top-line chat categories span the gamut and include topics like business, family, government, hobbies, sports, and relationships. A recent search on Yahoo! Groups list revealed the following chat room subcategories of adult content: divorce, extramarital affairs, gay, lesbian, bisexual, and swingers. Each of these categories can then have even more subcategories, getting more specific with each level down. Underneath the category of extramarital affairs, I found a group called *DiscreteDaytimePlaytime* that invites adults to apply for membership in a group that holds daytime orgies starting at noon and running until midnight, at various hotels in California. All a user needs to access a chat room or group like this is an account with the online provider. Thus, to gain access to the myriad of chat/ discussion rooms on MySpace, all a child needs is a MySpace account.

Chat rooms or groups are not places for minors to be hanging out. I can think of no logical reason to allow an impressionable young middle school child access to a chat room. *None*! There are too many risks associated with discussing hobbies, likes, dislikes, fetishes, and so on with strangers, some of whom may be sexual predators masquerading as others in the chat room to hone in on their next prey. For children that need special help or someone to talk to, I recommend consulting with your physician or school counselor to get a recommendation for a psychiatrist or psychologist. If you suspect your child is using chat rooms that are not being blocked by CyberPatrol, use PC Tattletale to monitor their online activities and block the services you find offensive.

Online Gaming: Additional Risk

One of the most common ways for kids to chat online is through the use of Internet-enabled computer games. Many parents with an elementary school child that has access to the Internet have heard of the game Runescape. My son used to play this and while seemingly harmless at the surface, it has embedded chat in the game that allows other users to pose questions to someone that they virtually walk up to in the course of playing the game. Kids need to know that games can be dangerous places as well and that they should never give out any personal information, including their real name, to anyone that asks in an online game. If these types of games present problems, simply add the appropriate Web site to the CyberPatrol blocked list, and your risk will be decreased.

MAKING PHONE CALLS OVER THE INTERNET

One of the biggest risks of using sophisticated IM tools is the ability to place phone calls directly over the Internet. Children can use their home computer and IM software to make phone calls to anyone in the world. Predators love this technology because they can use it to develop a more personal relationship with a potential victim and not tip off parents that the call or communication even took place. My recommendation is clear —unsupervised (and unlogged) voice calls over the Internet by children is a significant risk and should be mitigated. Blocking IM and sites that offer these tools is at the top of the list of recommendations in this chapter. Children will be much safer if they use their parent's home phone or their own cell phone to place calls to people they know. If parents allow their child to have a cell phone, they should monitor the call logs from their phone provider and turn off text messaging, especially for younger children.

HOW PREDATORS FIND THEIR VICTIMS

Sexual predators are smart. They know how to develop online relationships with impressionable children, and they definitely know which tools to use and how to do so effectively. There's not a single tool or approach that arms a sexual predator with enough information to exploit a child. They usually piece together bits of information to get additional personal data and then move in using a variety of tools that can include email, IM, chat, and VOIP. Today's kids expose too much information about themselves in a variety of online forums and sites. Figure 8.2 provides an example on how a predator can gain personal information using different tools.

The following approach is just one example of how a predator can get access to enough personal information from a child to be dangerous.

1. Search teen chat rooms masquerading as a teenager, looking for email addresses and IM screen names.
2. Search online member profiles of popular social networking sites for additional information by using a found email address or IM screen name. Search for posted pictures of the child and friends and if need be—cross-reference any information found about their posted friends.
3. Armed with an email address or IM screen name, use a search engine to find any references of a related home or cell phone number.
4. Search online directories for a home address that is affiliated with a phone number.
5. Using mapping and driving direction Web sites, search for a map and directions to the home address.
6. Using other powerful search databases, look up school names and addresses within the proximity to the home address.

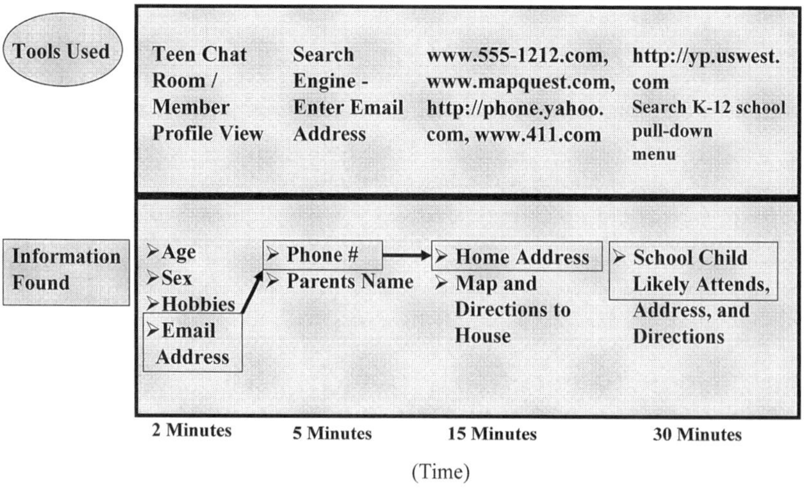

Tools Used	Teen Chat Room / Member Profile View	Search Engine - Enter Email Address	www.555-1212.com, www.mapquest.com, http://phone.yahoo. com, www.411.com	http://yp.uswest. com Search K-12 school pull-down menu
Information Found	➢ Age ➢ Sex ➢ Hobbies ➢ Email Address	➢ Phone # ➢ Parents Name	➢ Home Address ➢ Map and Directions to House	➢ School Child Likely Attends, Address, and Directions
	2 Minutes	5 Minutes	15 Minutes	30 Minutes

(Time)

Figure 8.2 How Predators Get Personal Information

Simply put, the tools on the Internet combined with a child or teenager that (unintentionally or intentionally) posts personal content about themselves on the Internet can be found relatively easily by a predator or anybody else. It's the parents' job to help mitigate these risks, and that takes knowledge, tools (like CyberPatrol and PC Tattletale), and the will to do something about it.

RECOMMENDATIONS

The following recommendations are provided to help parents guard against the risks and dangers associated with these technologies.

All Ages

- Lock down children's user accounts on home computers to prevent them from installing new software like IM or peer-to-peer communications programs on your computer.
- Install PC Tattletale on all laptops and enable stealth mode from time to time for middle and high school children. Review usage via the movie play-back feature as needed and remember to delete log files.

Category 1: Elementary School (Ages 8–11)

- Children in this age category should *not* have an IM account and should not be making unsupervised phone calls over the Internet. These tools are even more dangerous than email accounts and are the preferred method of communication by sexual predators. Use CyberPatrol to block chat and the following IM tool sites:

  - www.google.com/talk
  - http://aimexpress.aol.com
  - www.aim.com
  - www.yahoo.com/r/p1
  - http://messenger.yahoo.com
  - http://get.live.com
  - http://login.live.com
  - www.icq.com
  - http://download.icq.com
  - www.adiumx.com

- www.bitwiseim.com
- http://www.ceruleanstudios.com

- Block chat via CyberPatrol using the procedures outlined in this chapter.
- If needed, use PC Tattletale to see what you're kids are doing online and block their preferred IM tools and chat room sites as necessary by adding them to the CyberPatrol blocked list of sites and programs. CyberPatrol is an effective tool at blocking IM tools only after they've been installed on your home computer.

Category 2: Middle School (Ages 12–14)

- Children in this age category should *not* have an IM account and should definitely not be making unsupervised phone calls over the Internet. Duplicate the recommendation on this one from category 1, including the list of blocked sites and programs.
- Block chat and chat room sites via CyberPatrol using the procedures outlined in this chapter.
- If needed, use PC Tattletale to see what you're kids are doing online and block their preferred IM tools and chat room sites as necessary by adding them to the CyberPatrol blocked list of sites and programs.
- If parents do allow their children to use IM, enable PC Tattletale *all the time* and review the logs frequently. Also, teach children to *never* publish their IM screen name on any public Web site or social networking site. Predators use these bits of information to hunt down their next potential victim.

Category 3: High School (Ages 15–17)

- Children in this age category will likely have an IM account to be social and fit in at school. Parents need to reinforce that IM is a privilege and if misused, it can be taken away. Standardize on just one IM tool and monitor your children by using PC Tattletale for inappropriate behavior or use.
- Recommend to your teenager that they do not use away messages with their IM tool. Away messages are popular with teens as they're a way of telling their friends what they are feeling, where they are, and so on. Unfortunately, these type of messages advertise too much information about them and add risk.

- Block chat rooms via CyberPatrol by using a combination of programs and blocked sites. Chat rooms are not for children of any age.
- Expose your mature teenagers to some of the risks associated on the Internet in plain terms. Teach them to *never* publish their IM screen name or favorite chat rooms on any public Web site or social networking site. Predators use these bits of information to hunt down their next potential victim.
- Put in place a family policy of no Internet phone calls and monitor via PC Tattletale. If a teenager break the rules, warn once, then block their IM tool with CyberPatrol's program restriction feature. Unsupervised phone calls with strangers on the Internet should not be allowed for any child, including teenagers.

Cell Phones and PDAs

Technology is dominated by two types of people: those who understand what they do not manage, and those who manage what they do not understand.

—Putt's Law

AN OVERVIEW OF PORTABLE COMMUNICATION DEVICES

Cell phones are the hot tool for most kids, and the devices have evolved to include many of the software components and features on standard computers. Global growth in the adoption of cell phones has exploded in the past decade or so, and is accelerating at an even more rapid rate in developing countries like India and China, where technology is redefining how people interact with one another. Over 1 billion mobile phones were shipped in 2006, a 22.5 percent increase from 2005.[1] Today's cell phones can really be broken down into the following four categories.

1. Child/restricted phones
2. Standard cellular phones
3. PDAs
4. Satellite phones

Child/restricted phones come in a variety of flavors, but all of them greatly limit what the phone holder can do. Most of these phones have a limited number of keys that restrict the number of phone numbers the user can call. They also restrict most other add-ons like downloading games or text messaging. Some of the phone providers in this category have built in global positioning system (GPS) capabilities that allow parents to find out where exactly their children are or where they placed their last call from. (I will discuss vendor and products in more detail later.) These types of phones are really simple phones that children can use to get a hold of a parent, teacher, or guardian in the event of an emergency.

Standard cell phones are what most teenagers and parents currently use. They offer a variety of features and add-ons, but the primary purpose of the device is to make phone calls. Some of the add-ons that are cool but add risk to children include instant messaging, Internet browsing, email, text messaging, cameras, and video camcorders. The majority of standard cell phones have 10-key phone pads that are fine for making calls but clunky for sending text or email messages. Many providers are now integrating MP3 players into their phones as more teenagers opt for listening to music as well as making phone calls.

PDAs (personal digital assistants) are used mainly by working professionals who need voice, email, and integrated calendars, contacts, and address books that are essential to managing their professional career and home environment. I use one of these devices and find it invaluable. The breakdown of features that I use most often on my PDA is as follows: 50 percent email, 30 percent voice calls, and 20 percent calendar activity—all of which is wirelessly synchronized with my email and calendar system at work. These devices are usually much more expensive in terms of initial purchase price and come with higher monthly usage fees for voice and data. Even though teens find PDAs attractive, they should be used for business purposes and are not ideal for children due to the number of features that can add risk.

Satellite phones are the last category of phones. They are the high-end version of communication intended for international travelers who must stay in contact anywhere on the globe. I've used these phones many times in my professional career, mostly to stay in contact with staff and colleagues at work and with family at home from remote locations like Nepal, Bhutan, Africa, and several locations in South America. Satellite phones are very expensive, ranging in price between $1000 and $2000, and require monthly service plans for per-minute usage. These are clearly not for children. Satellite phones are an option for the business elite and professionals that work in far off places with poor in-country communications systems.

Now I'll cover the types of functions that are readily available on phones and PDAs. The following describes the main features. Users can

- make voice calls and access voicemail where necessary
- download and play music (sometimes for a fee)
- download and play games
- browse the Internet
- manage contacts and calendars
- download various ring tones (usually for a fee)
- send and receive email. Many phones and PDAs have email programs built into them, and others allow users to download specialized email program add-ons from vendors like Google.
- send and receive text messages (SMS) to other phones
- push-to-talk two-way radio capability (certain models/networks)
- chat with other users. Chatting is essentially sending small text messages to one another over the Internet. Chatting requires both parties to be connected to the Internet and available using the same instant messaging (IM) tool to communicate.
- take, send, and receive photographs. Some carriers charge separate fees for sending photos via email, while others do not. Don't forget to read the fine print on your contract.
- view video files (downloaded or streamed)
- record video files and send them to other users. Most phone providers that have an integrated camera also provide for users to take short video clips, save them for future viewing, and send them to others as desired.

Considering all of these features, are the risks as high as with these features on a computer? Parents often see kids using text messaging, email, and browsing the Internet directly from their phone, and might assume that there must not be any risk associated with these devices. Because phones are mobile and in many ways used away from one's parents, they are actually *more* risky with a full feature set than similar tools on a desktop or laptop. The following list shows top threats associated with children using cell phones.

1. Cell phones have become the target of advertising with companies peddling their wares via text messages and email to cell phone users. That means getting advertisements for content that may be inappropriate for children.
2. Email accounts on a phone are more difficult for parents to monitor and screen. In addition, anti-spam tools and parental controls on phones are nowhere near as good as the protection available for computers today.
3. Monitoring software hasn't caught up to the mobile environment yet.

There isn't a PC Tattletale version for a phone at the moment, but it may be coming. Parents are at the cell phone provider's mercy when it comes to providing reports and appropriate content filters. The telecommunications industry in general is notorious for being behind on these kinds of technologies. They often roll out trendy new features and then think about security after the fact. It's a revenue game for this industry, not a safety focus.

4. IM software on a cell phone opens up the risk of hidden and nonlogged conversations between friends and potential sexual predators. Remember, IM is the preferred hidden tool of communication because many of the conversations are not logged. As consistent with my recommendation in Chapter 8, just say no to IM on the phone, too.

5. Internet access via a cell phone is a parent's nightmare and a huge risk for children, plain and simple. Most cell phone providers don't have parental controls for phones, and the ones that do have significant disclaimers on their Web site indicating that they may not work well. My tests revealed that most cell phones with Internet access provide an open portal to pretty much any content on the Internet. I even tested my BlackBerry's Internet access and was able to get to adult sites with pictures quite easily.

6. Camera and video capabilities are a risk on a phone if a child misuses the feature. Phones with email or IM capability can also display pictures and videos sent to the user. This means that there's an opportunity that a child may receive an email or picture from a stranger that contains pornography or other inappropriate content.

7. Cell phones and some of the add-ons, like IM and text messaging, can be very expensive for parents and teens if they don't pay attention to how their phone service provider charges for them. Most phone companies have discounted the cost of voice calls to within 2.5 to 5 cents per minute in the United States. At that rate, they're not making much money off of their customer. Thus, they bring in the add-ons. Text messaging can cost 15 cents per message, over 10 times the cost of a one-minute call. Parents need to restrict these types of extra fees and only provide the features their children need to stay in touch.

How Cell Phones Work and Where GPS Fits In

A cell phone is essentially a basic device and radio that contains a low-power transmitter which communicates via a series of towers and base stations.[2] Phones get their signal from the nearest cell tower, and as customers move from one area to another, one tower transfers the signal to the nearest one with a stronger signal.[3] Buildings and confined areas within them, like elevators, can present problems for cell phones because they can't find and connect to a tower and antenna with a strong enough signal. That's why people often drop calls in the center of large buildings or underground subway tunnels—there's no signal strong enough to carry the call through. The only way to guarantee a signal in areas like these is for the provider to install antennas inside those remote areas. Some corporations install such devices to ensure that their staff can get clear phone calls and send and receive email. When you're operating in a wireless environment, the nearest tower is king.

Cell phones with GPS capabilities also rely on radio waves, but instead of looking for the nearest ground-based tower, they look to the sky for the closest satellite orbiting the Earth.[4] Some cell phone service providers (like Sprint) have launched GPS location features with their phone, which allow parents to locate their children with the phone via satellite within a pretty good level of a accuracy—usually 100 to 500 yards.[5] To determine the location of a GPS phone holder, the GPS receiver has to determine the location of at least three satellites and then uses trilateration to determine the exact location, latitude and longitude, of the phone.[6] Some GPS phones use other methods to determine the location of the phone, including the use of satellites in conjunction with information about the cell phone's signal.[7] This is sometimes called enhanced GPS or wireless GPS and can often get a faster fix on the phone than just satellite-based approaches alone.[8] Sophisticated PDAs and cell phones with support for Java programming languages can actually turn them into navigational devices and provide nearly real-time driving instructions.[9] In any event, GPS phones are here to stay and are a valuable tool for parents who want to track their children's location.

Options on the Market Today

In an attempt to slice through the promotional material on phones, I've researched and recommended a number of phones and services that will help parents. I list them for each of the phone categories defined earlier. The following options are available for parents as they decide which technology to let their children use when it comes to phones.

Child/Restricted Phones

1. Firefly (www.fireflymobile.com)

   - $80 purchase price with service plans starting at $9.99/month
   - Five-key phone with no standard keypad, no contract, cancel any time

- Emergency button requires network access and works even if the phone is out of minutes
- Parental controls for incoming and outgoing phone numbers
- No GPS locator capability

2. Tictalk (www.tictalk.com)

   - $99 purchase price with various service plans
   - Download photos
   - Stop watch
   - Learning games included with points system for playing them
   - Parental controls for incoming and outgoing phone numbers

3. Wherifone (www.wherify.com)

   - $99 purchase price with various service plans starting at $20/month
   - World's smallest GPS locator capability and tracking phone
   - Parents can find phone location via the Web or another phone
   - Shows street and aerial maps and can automatically capture locations at preset times and days
   - No games or text messaging
   - 20-number phone book
   - SOS panic/emergency button, requires network access and works even if the phone is out of minutes
   - Parental controls for incoming and outgoing phone numbers

Standard Cell Phone Providers

1. Sprint GPS Locator phones (https://sfl.sprintpcs.com/finder-sprint-family/signIn.htm)

   - $99 and higher purchase price with various service plans for voice and data
   - GPS locator feature allows parents can find phone location via the Web or another phone (30+ phones to choose from)
   - Email, text messaging (SMS)
   - Bluetooth wireless to work with hands-free headsets
   - Push-to-talk two-way radio (on certain models)
   - View videos
   - Sound recorder

- Java capable—allows other types of programs, such as turn-by-turn navigation
- MP3 audio player
- Internet browsing on certain phones

2. Other GPS and non-GPS provider cell phones (AT&T, T-Mobile, etc.)

PDAs (Usually Include Fully Functional QWERTY Keypads)

1. BlackBerry (www.blackberry.com)
2. Nokia (www.nokia.com)
3. T-Mobile (www.t-mobile.com)
4. Sony Ericsson (www.sonyericsson.com)
5. Apple iPhone (www.apple.com)

Satellite Phones

1. Iridium (www.iridium.com)

As you can see from the features list in the standard cell phone category, there are a lot to choose from, complicating a parent's choice and also adding risk to a child or teenager. Most of the phones in this category don't offer GPS capabilities, so if you're interested in a phone service that has a program to track the user via GPS satellite and tower-based services, you need to ensure that the phone you purchase has that function.

Advanced PDAs offer many features and are designed to be good voice phones and excellent email communicators. Many of these devices allow for IM plug-ins so that users can maintain one IM service and screen name, regardless of whether they're communicating from their PDA or their computer. These sophisticated devices also usually have fully functioning Internet browsers and not stripped-down text versions like earlier devices. Email programs supported are also usually productive and some come with slimmed-down versions of Outlook. These are not worth the risk of trying to manage for children and are often too expensive anyway.

One Last Alternative for Pre-Phone Communication

Parents who have children in elementary school they want to keep track of have another slick option available on the market, but it that doesn't quite fit into the cell phone category. Two-way pagers allow parents to keep tabs on their kids within a short distance, usually one to two miles, and may work well when their children are playing outside their home or at a park. Two-way pagers have been around for years and are effective, low-cost devices. They don't however provide GPS tracking capabilities, just instant communication.

A recent newcomer to the two-way radio market is the Wristwatch Communicator from XACT. It's a pretty cool watch with a rugged case and digital screen that comes equipped with a small talk button below the watch dial.[10] The XACT Communicator retails for about $45 (it can be purchased online for about half that), requires no monthly service, is voice activated, and can communicate over a range of 22 channels to a distance reliably within a mile or two.[11] Thus, for parents who don't want to plunk down the cash for a moderately priced kid-friendly phone with service or a more expensive standard cell phone, this is a great option, especially in the early elementary school years. My wife found this device on the Internet in the course of researching less expensive tools for parents.

TEXT MESSAGING: HOW TEENS COMMUNICATE

Ok—time for a reality moment. Teens prefer to communicate via text messaging (SMS) because they think it's cool, discreet (their phone doesn't ring), and they can hide much of what they're saying from their parents. Texting has some risks, and it's an uphill battle for parents to fight. According to the Cellular Telecommunications and Internet Association, the number of text messages sent per month from 2001 to 2005 grew from a little over 14 million to 2.5 billion.[12] Keep in mind that many of the cell phone service providers like AT&T, Qwest, Sprint, and T-Mobile don't just let these messages fly from phone to phone without charging a fee. Fees can be incorporated into the monthly service charge for the phone, charged via a flat fee, say, for up to 200 messages per month, or individually at a high cost, up to 15 cents per message. The reality is that text messages are here to stay. Though not appropriate for younger children, text messaging will be a method of communication for your teenager.

MONITORING CALL LOGS AND BILLS

Because phones are mobile in nature, move in and out of the household, and can be pretty much controlled by the user, then need to be proactively monitored. Tricks teens might use to conceal their phone activities include the following.

1. Deleting sent and received text messages
2. Deleting the list of recent phone calls made
3. Taking photographs or short videos, emailing them to friends, and then deleting the audit trail of the message
4. If enabled, browsing adult-oriented Web sites on their phone and emailing some of the more interesting ones to their friends as links

As stated earlier, monitoring software and controls for computers aren't readily available for cell phones. This will become a growth market, and one that adult consumers will likely drive in the coming years. Today parents are at the mercy of logging and reporting capabilities from their cell phone service providers. I encourage all parents purchasing standard cell phones for their children to inquire about the types of monitoring and usage reports that can be delivered to them before buying the phone. If you're not comfortable with usage reporting (or lack thereof), you should greatly restrict the types of services on your children's phone. The recommendations section of this chapter provides some clear guidance in this area with regard to what features to allow and for what age category.

BROWSING AND IM CHALLENGES WITH PDAs

Children of all ages should *not* have a cell phone with an Internet browser. There really isn't any need for one, and the risks are too great. Cell phones should be used for voice calls, not browsing. I guarantee that they won't be researching web sites for homework on a cell phone with an Internet connection, so why give it to them. Blocking this feature will also keep them out of online chat rooms and social networking sites from their phone, if they are not be blocked by your cell phone service provider. This typically drives up the cost of the monthly service, as most vendors charge a fixed fee per month or by the amount of data , usually in megabytes, that is transferred through the network. In my professional career, I've rarely found a need for an Internet browser on my phone, but there are some businesses that use them to keep their employees in touch with key information via special programs designed for their PDA. Do yourself and favor and sleep better at night by keeping the Internet connections available for your children restricted to computers in your home, school, and libraries, where they can be better protected and monitored.

To close this section out, keep those nasty IM programs off of kid's cell phones, too. Remember, IM is a predator's preferred mode of communication because most of the messages are not logged by the individual users themselves.

Effective cell phones for middle and high school children have the following key features that most kids can live with.

- Voice calls
- Text messaging (for mature teens)
- Email (for responsible teens)
- MP3 players

Everything else comes with risk and isn't necessary.

RECOMMENDATIONS

The following recommendations are provided to help parents be effective with these risky technologies. As with prior chapters, recommendations are broken down by age category.

Category 1: Elementary School (Ages 8–11)

- Children in this age category should *not* have a cell phone. I recognize that there will be some exceptions, so for working parents who feel strongly that their child should have one in case of emergencies, select one of the child/restricted phones with limited services and keys, but ensure that it has GPS and the feature, possibly a locator service, is turned on. GPS can be a helpful tool if kids are missing.

For parents who insist on a cell phone for their elementary school child, follow these recommendations.

- Block text messaging (incoming and outgoing) and IM by contacting the cell phone service provider.
- Block Internet browsing by calling the cell phone service provider. The parental controls for cell phones today are not good, and many don't protect against adult content. *No child* should have a cell phone with Internet browsing. The risks are too great.
- Block email capabilities by contacting the cell phone service provider. This recommendation is consistent with not allowing elementary school children to have an email account.
- Purchase a cell phone that doesn't have a camera. They are unnecessary add-ons, and children in this age bracket will use them as toys.

- An alternative to a cell phones for this age category is a two-way radio or communicator, such as the Wristwatch Communicator from XACT. These devices cost less than cell phones, don't require monthly service plans, and are perfect for parents who want to keep in touch with their child as he or she plays outside with friends. They have a range of about 1 to 2 miles.

Category 2: Middle School (Ages 12–14)

- Purchase a cell phone from the standard cell phones category and ensure that it has a GPS capability that is turned on. I like what Sprint has to offer and believe that they've taken the lead on providing this valuable technology in the marketplace. GPS and locator Web-based and phone-based tracking add-ons can be especially helpful when keeping tabs on active teenagers and can come in handy if a child goes missing.
- I recommend that parents pay for their child's first cell phone, but consider having their children pay for a portion of the monthly usage bill. I've done this with my children and have found that it teaches kids responsibility and that people should work for the things that they want. From my perspective—nothing is free and if it is, it won't last forever.
- If desired, enable text messaging (incoming and outgoing), but review the text logs from time to time by asking to see the phone or calling the service provider and requesting a detailed usage report. Children at this age will likely press their parents for a phone that allows text messaging because it's the preferred way of communication for young teens. If your child receives unsolicited text messages from strangers, consider disabling the feature.
- Block IM by contacting the cell phone service provider. Parents should inspect the phone every few months to ensure that their children haven't downloaded and installed a free IM add-on for their phone. If they have, reinforce the rules with a warning and, if necessary, revoke the phone for repeat offenders.
- Block Internet browsing by calling the cell phone service provider. *No child* should have a cell phone with Internet browsing.
- Block email capabilities by contacting the service provider. For children at this age, email on a phone is a luxury. The primary purpose of a phone is to call someone, especially if there is an emergency. Don't lose sight of that purpose. Because parental controls and anti-spam measures aren't as good on phones as they are on computers, it's not worth exposing middle

school children to those risks. They should be happy with voice calls and text messaging.

- If parents purchase a phone with a built-in camera, they need to have a serious conversation with their child about the risks and acceptable use. Tell them the real life story about how students in New Jersey were expelled for taking pictures of other students and teachers and posting them to the Internet.
- Children at this age should *not* have a PDA. They're more expensive, usually come packed with additional features, and are not suited for children. Leave them to the working professionals.
- Add the following Web sites to CyberPatrol's blocked site list to prevent children from downloading mobile email and IM programs that can work on their phones:

  - http://mobile.google.com
  - http://sms.google.com
  - www.google.com/mobile/gmail
  - http://download.icq.com/download/icq2go
  - *http://mobile.yahoo.com*

Chapter 8 covers how to block Skype, which works for mobile phones as well. Unfortunately, there are too many other free mobile email programs to list in this chapter.

- Look at your child's phone from time to time and see what free add-on programs have been added. PC Tattletale may come in handy because most of these programs have to be downloaded to a computer before they can be installed on a phone. This is one other good reason to *not* allow Internet browsing from the phone itself, as teens can download any programs that work with their phone as they see fit.

Category 3: High School (Ages 15–17)

- Purchase a cell phone from the standard cell phones category and ensure that it has a GPS capability that is turned on. GPS and locator Web-based and phone-based tracking add-ons can be especially helpful when keeping tabs on active teenagers and can come in handy if a child goes missing.
- I recommend that parents pay for their child's first cell phone, but consider having their teenagers pay for a portion (possibly all) of the monthly usage

bill. Teens at this age should also pay for any phone upgrades and accessories. It teaches them responsibility at an appropriate age, and most teens are able to find some kind of work to earn money for the latest styling phone that they've just got to have. These are luxury items, not necessities.

- Enable text messaging (incoming and outgoing), but review the text logs from time to time by asking to see the phone or calling the service provider and requesting a detailed usage report. If your teenager receives unsolicited text messages from strangers, consider disabling the feature.
- Block IM and Internet browsing by calling the cell phone service provider.
- Enable email capabilities by calling the service provider and ensure that the provider turn on anti-spam features. If they don't have an anti-spam offering for their email function, then disable the feature. Spam and the varieties that they come in, including adult content, are not appropriate for any teenager.
- If you purchase a phone with a built-in camera, you need to have a serious conversation with your teen about acceptable use.
- Add the following Web sites to CyberPatrol's blocked site list to prevent children from downloading mobile email and IM programs that can work on their phones:

  - http://mobile.google.com
  - http://sms.google.com

  Unfortunately, there are too many other free mobile email programs to list in this chapter.
- Look at your child's phone from time to time and see what free add-on programs have been added. PC Tattletale may also come in handy because most of these programs have to be downloaded to a computer before they can be installed on a phone. This is one other good reason to *not* allow Internet browsing from the phone itself because teens can download any programs that work with their phone as they see fit.
- Children at this age should *not* have a professional PDA. Again, they're best suited for adults, not children.
- Review your child's cell phone bill from time to time to see who they are communicating with, who they call versus who calls them, and how long the calls are. If there are odd or repeating entries, confront your child immediately and ask questions.

A Glimpse into the Future

The best way to predict the future is to invent it.

—Alan Kay

CONVERGING DEVICES

It's already starting to happen. Internet-enabled devices are rapidly proliferating in the marketplace, and vendors are rushing to produce and market products that have wired or wire-free access to the Internet. PCs with access to the Web have evolved to other, smaller, and more personal devices like cell phones, PDAs, and even watches. Television and media companies are also embracing the Internet as they look for alternatives to standard TV and cable programs to get content and advertisements to consumers.

At the end of the day, the devices on the market will converge in terms of features, but they will also expand in numbers of various types. Cell phones will evolve into high-end PDAs and will be fully packed with features, leaving a void of simpler devices for parents to chose from. Innovation and experimentation in today's businesses and academic institutions will result in a more competitive market. Multinational product-based firms with enough cash and market presence will buy up small and innovative companies and build them into their portfolio. There will continue to be rapid acceleration of technical innovations and a reduction in size of wireless devices.

FREE STUFF EVERYWHERE (ADVERTISERS' HEAVEN)

Advertisers are moving from traditional print media and into the electronic space with a focus on any delivery mechanism to get to a customer or prospect. You have undoubtedly seen the advertisements that proliferate most Internet home pages and Web portals. There are very few major Internet portal sites (if any at all) that don't offer some form of advertisements. I just clicked on four such sites: MSN.com, Yahoo.com, CNN.com, and AOL.com, and not one of them came up add free. As I'm writing this, I just got a SPAM email to start a nursing degree as well. What accuracy . . .

One of the problems with advertisements for consumers is that many of them are not targeted toward what the recipient is looking for. Some advertisers use sophisticated analytics and pore over Web site click-stream analysis, like Amazon.com does, to offer up links to content or products that they think are related to ones that the consumer has viewed or previously purchased. Those are the good guys. The bad advertisers use a variety of mediums including email, text messaging, voice calls, Web pages, and direct mail to peddle their wares, many of which are not appropriate for children. Some categorize these vendors as spammers because the unwanted email is just one part of the other electronic media used in these campaigns. Regardless of the current scope of advertising, it's here to stay and will likely get more prevalent as we see more decentralized and personal computing devices tapped into the Internet. That said, parents are cautioned against adopting technologies that don't provide appropriate filters to remove or restrict content from getting to their children.

GLOBAL POSITIONING TAKES OFF

Global positioning systems (GPS) will become a household word with most mobile items that connect to the Internet having some kind of GPS real-time and static locator functionality. In the next decade or so, GPS will be available on such items as cars, bikes, watches, phones, jewelry, and other accessories in an effort to locate and track people and things around the world. Software services to support these items will become mature and will be accessible from a variety of devices, not just computers with Web access. Get ready for a society that tracks everything from customers to criminals via GPS.

BUILT-IN SECURITY FOR FUTURE OPERATING SYSTEMS

Operating systems that control home computers, laptops, and servers will get better at securing the environment and data within. Some of the best operating systems of prior years were more closed in nature and had to be opened via configuration to expose security risks. Today's operating systems are quite the opposite, requiring technology professionals to harden or close them to prevent hackers from exposing weaknesses in them and gaining access to private information or even taking control of the host computer itself.

Tomorrow's operating systems will be better secured and move from a decentralized model back to a centralized model in some form of large hosting on the Internet via a private or public access with encryption playing a key role. Many of the software utilities and add-ons that help secure predominantly Windows-based decentralized computers will be purchased by the largest companies and integrated into the operating system. As a result, the services sector that provides for much of these add-on security services will diminish, and software vendors that stay in business will focus on nonsecurity types of applications instead.

FUTURISTIC WAYS TO STAY CONNECTED

If I had a crystal ball that would help me predict the future, I could help a lot of people and make a lot of money! Unfortunately, there is no such orb that can forecast where we'll end up in 5, 10, and 20 years. What we have to rely on is past information, trend forecasting, and plain old gut feelings based on the types of technology inventions and innovations we think will be introduced and will survive the marketplace. Before I provide some of my predictions, I thought I'd share some from others.

> People's social networks will be richer and more interesting, but the closest parts of those networks won't be numerically larger—we can only take in about 150 people, virtually or in real space. . . . [1] Susan Crawford, professor, Cardozo School of Law/Policy Fellow with the Center for Democracy & Technology/Fellow with the Yale Law School Information Society Project

> By 2014, as telework and home-schooling expand, the boundaries between work and leisure will diminish significantly. This will sharply alter everyday family dynamics. . . . [2]

> It is 2025. Your mobile is now much more than just a communication device—more like a remote control on your life. On a typical day, it will start working even before you wake. . . . [3] Dr. William Webb, head of Research and Development at the regulator Ofcom

> Most access to the Internet will be via wireless networks, especially as cities begin to establish WiFi grids. Just as many Americans are foregoing their land-lines at home for cell phones, I suspect that they will give up their broadband for wireless. . . . [4] A. Halavais, State University of New York at Buffalo

At least one devastating attack will occur in the next 10 years on the networked information infrastructure or the country's power grid.[5]

The following are my own predictions regarding technologies that will impact parents, children, and society in general in the coming years.

By 2010

- Personal privacy on the Internet will continue to erode. More access will be in the form of wireless mechanisms, resulting in more of our activities being captured into some kind of marketing or government database.
- Boundaries between work and home life will continue to blur as a result of technology integration in professional and consumer devices. Societies and countries that embrace this trend the most will be the most productive labor markets on the planet at the risk of increasing health problems resulting from stress and other technology impairments that we haven't determined yet.
- Cell phones and PDAs will fully converge and prices will fall so that almost anyone wanting a full-featured device can have one, leaving very few basic options for consumers. Standard features will include streaming audio/video, email, IM, text messaging, MP3 player, Internet access, games, voice recorders, calendars, to do lists, and full-function video players. Disk storage systems for these devices will expand from current limitations of 40–80 GB to 500 GB to 1 terabyte, and screen resolution for all activities will be crystal clear and comparable to HDTV.
- Email will become fully integrated with voicemail systems, and users will be able to either read their messages or listen to them via their cell phone. These systems are evolving and available today for business customers, and will be consumer-ready at a relatively low cost in the future.
- Social networking will continue to evolve with an increase in the number of online interactions and a decrease of the quality of those interactions. Today's social networking sites list thousands of friends for each person registered. Those friends aren't really friends by nature, just those wishing to be engaged online in some form or frequency of communication. Trusting online relationships will continue to be low in number and will only increase as real-time video chatting and other more interactive forms of communication improves current forms of interaction like email, IM, and text messaging.
- Miniature external sound-reducing headsets and earphones will become

common, allowing phone users to talk with other background noises almost totally eliminated for the party on the other end. These technologies are just starting to appear on the market and are expected to be fully incorporated in phones and wireless headsets in the mass market shortly.

- Anti-virus, anti-spam, and parental controls will greatly improve for the cell phone industry, allowing parents to adjust with much better granularity the types of content their children see and hear on their mobile device. Current on/off controls will be replaced and driven by software vendors that have developed solutions for laptops and desktop computers.
- Major search engines will consolidate as competition increases for both advertising revenue and unique Web site visitors.
- GPS will become standard in cell phone and mobile device technology as compared to just a select number of devices currently offering GPS location services today.
- The Internet and TV will converge. Viewing programs, watching movies, and accessing the Internet will be done through a variety of devices in the family room and not just via computers and PDAs.
- Intelligent watches with Internet features will begin to emerge again. The initial round of techno-looking devices will be replaced by stylish options from reputable jewelers, not computer manufacturers.
- Productivity office software, like Microsoft Office, will be accessible via an Internet subscription instead of relying on program downloads to individual computers. These applications will be accessible via an Internet portal by users, regardless of the device from which they are connecting, and storage for information will be hosted on the Internet instead of stored within individual decentralized devices.
- The adult pornography industry will be as robust as ever, offering a wide array of content (teaser and subscription) via a variety of Internet-enabled devices. Real-time video camera functionality will evolve from computers to smaller devices like PDAs, enabling mobile interactive sessions and viewing.

By 2015

- IP version 6 will be fully integrated into society, allowing just about any electronic device to have a unique IP address and connect to the Internet.
- A significant percentage of the world will have access to the Internet in

some way. The proliferation of inexpensive portable communication devices will facilitate the increase.

- Security and access to devices and systems will be driven by biometrics instead of character-entered passwords.
- Voice calls over the Internet will merge with traditional phone vendors and wireless offerings. Phones will evolve to accommodate automatically switching between multiple paths to place a voice call, including those that travel over land lines, wireless cell towers, satellites, and Internet connections.
- GPS tracking capabilities will be embedded into much smaller objects such as watches, jewelry, pens, purses, and wallets, giving parents greater control with monitoring and keeping their children safe.
- Brick-and-mortar book and video stores will diminish if not be gone from the marketplace. Customers will be able to purchase and wirelessly transfer content to an Internet-enabled wearable device via a variety of mechanisms, including in a store or from other point-of-purchase portals. Thus, retail stores for electronic media may exist, but they will probably offer virtual products instead of stocking the shelves with physical products. Wireless installations will become the gold standard going forward.
- Email and text messaging will morph toward full voice message delivery via wireless and nearly invisible ear plugs that will replace awkward looking Bluetooth wireless earphones.
- Cell phone QWERTY email keyboards will be augmented by speech recognition software that will allow users to record messages and send/receive them as a voice calls.
- Mobile devices will evolve to controlling other devices in the home and office via wireless applications and add-ons. Capabilities include remote controlling home devices (TVs, DVDs, stereos, etc.) and being able to ubiquitously print documents via built-in wireless printing without additional add-on software.
- Refrigerators and other appliances will have Internet-enabled inventory systems built in and use scanning technology to automatically place orders over the Internet for items that need to be replaced.

By 2025

- Internet bandwidth will increase to homes and businesses by a factor of 100, facilitating the migration away from decentralized devices like PCs to Internet appliances, with information stored away from the actual device.

- Information-gathering activities from vendors for goods purchased, used, viewed, and accessed will proliferate into giant repositories of information that will blur what people intend to keep private and public.
- Advertisements will proliferate every electronic device connected to the Internet and will be served up and driven by what the consumer buys, sees, drives by, calls, emails, samples, and so on. Leading industrialized governments will have access to all of this information as part of a national intelligence program in support of national security. What people do will be tracked in these databases.
- The personal computer as we know it today will cease to exist and will be replaced by numerous consumer and professional devices integrated into the Internet.
- Holograms and three-dimensional graphics capabilities will be integrated into mobile devices for viewing various types of information, such as email, calendars, real-time video conferences, and person-to-person video feeds.

RECOMMENDATIONS

This is a difficult section to write given some of the predictions above. The following is the only advice I have at this point.

- In the next few years, don't fly on the cutting edge of technology, especially for consumer-related devices. They're usually too expensive at their launch and often don't live up to their marketing promise. The difficulty here is that children always seem to want the latest and greatest new gadget—especially if it is computer-related and allows them to communicate with friends. Hold the line or make them pay for it, but only after checking on the security and parental controls for those devices.
- As new kinds of technology come out that provide access to a variety of information, stay focused on what you choose to adopt. Remember that it's always a buyer's market from a technology perspective. Thus, let your children be kids at early ages, and don't rush to get them tech-savvy.
- Technology in the future will be even more decentralized than it is now, with literally thousands of types of products and devices tied to the Internet. As new kinds of services come online, try before you buy and *always* inquire about parental controls. If they don't have any or they're not fully vetted, take a pass and watch to see how others who do take the plunge fare. Early adopters of Internet-related devices might be introducing unknown risk to children—plain and simple.

Talking to Your Kids about Online Risks

Parents were invented to make children happy by giving them something to ignore.
—Ogden Nash

AN INTERNET USAGE CONTRACT

Part of parenting around technology is developing and setting clear expectations and rules. My parents did so, and I've adopted a similar approach with my kids. I can still remember my father's statement to me after I was all grown up:– "I gave you just enough rope to hang yourself." I interpreted that as giving me some freedom, clearly setting expectations, and explaining what would happen if I broke the rules. One summer when I was a kid, many of the teenage boys in my neighborhood started to experiment with taking their fathers' cars out for joy rides. Assuming that I wouldn't get into an accident, I thought through the other potential repercussions. Would my father know? Would he ground me? Would he let me drive when I became the legal age or make me wait for a few months or even a year? After thinking about these types of questions, I realized that he probably *would* know, probably by the way I would have parked his car back in the garage, and I would have gotten in some *serious* trouble. Thus, I never did it.

Only a few months later did I realize I made the right decision. One of the other boys in the neighborhood decided to take his father's car out for a spin. He lost control of the car and flipped it end over end, but fortunately he didn't injure himself. He also didn't get his license when the rest of us did because of his mistake. Parenting is about getting the right mix of love, learning, education, and toughness.

I encourage parents to set up an Internet contract with their children, especially middle school and high school teenagers. A contract signed by each child does three things: (1) clearly spells out expectations, and (2) puts in writing tips to help them stay safe, and (3) discusses repercussions of they break the rules. There are a variety of good contracts available on the Internet from sites like Netsmartz.org. My suggested contract would be a pledge that would be signed by each child and his or her parents/guardian and read like the following.

Internet Safety Agreement

1. **Personal Data**: I will *never* share private information on the Internet, which includes full name, address, Social Security number, phone number(s), school attended/attending, and recent pictures. Exceptions require approval from my parents.
2. **Talking with my Parents**: I promise to tell my parents about any strange things that come up as a result of using the Internet via email, IM, browsing, text messaging, social networking sites, and cell phone calls. If I feel uncomfortable as a result of using the Internet, I will talk to my parents, show them what made me feel strange, and listen to their advice on how to prevent the situation in the future.
3. **Banned Technology**: I promise *not* to use the following technology without first getting my parents' approval: (1) voice calls over the Internet, (2) instant messaging, (3) social networking sites, and (4) video cameras or Webcams. In addition, I will *never* (5) attempt to access adult/pornographic content, (6) enter a chat room, or (7) illegally copy or download material including games, songs, and videos that are not clearly advertised as free to the public.
4. **Dealing with Strangers**: I will *never* respond to an email message, text message, IM request, or phone call from a stranger (or someone that I don't know). I will also *never* agree to meet anyone that I've met on the Internet. I understand that people aren't always who they say they are.
5. **Respecting Others**: I will respect other people on the Internet that I communicate with and treat them as I wish to be treated.
6. **Breaking the Rules**: I understand that if I break these rules, that I may temporarily or permanently lose the right to use Internet technologies including email, browsing, cell phone, and text messaging. These tools are a privilege and not a right.

_____ Child's Signature Date _____

_____Parent's Signature Date_____

Feel free to use this template or mix and match the terms and conditions that work best for your family based on input and agreements from other reputable safety organizations outlined in this text.

WHEN AND HOW TO BE FIRM

Speaking to children about the risks of the Internet, rules of engagement, and repercussions can be difficult. Every child is different and they comprehend information differently at various age groups. The Web site Talk With Your Kids (www.talkingwithkids.org) has some good advice for talking to children about a variety of tough issues. Here are some other ideas.

1. Tell your children what's acceptable and what's *not* acceptable behavior on the Internet.
2. Set clear expectations and spell out penalties if they don't play by the rules.
3. Don't back down if they break the rules. Kids are notorious for wearing down parents.
4. Initiate conversations with your child if you sense something is wrong or if their behavior is changing. Don't wait for them to come to you.[1]
5. Listen to your child before enforcing a penalty. An infraction of the rules may not have been intentional or their fault. When you have all the facts, make the call. Reacting without listening is careless.
6. Be honest and patient. If you're disappointed with their actions, tell them why. If you change the rules or revoke a privilege, spell out the reasons, update their Internet agreement, and get them to sign it.[2]

WHAT NOT TO SAY TO YOUR TEEN

Talking to your kids about the risks of the Internet can be tricky. In addition, when dealing with kids that break the rules outlined in your Internet agreement, it's easy to get angry, express dissatisfaction with their actions, and say things that you may regret later. I offer the following advice on what *not* to say to your child as you implement an Internet safety approach.

- Speak to the age of your children. When discussing the risks of the Internet with your younger kids, be honest, tell them that you care about their safety, and give them examples of the risks. Inform them, don't scare them. Gory scare tactics are not appropriate for younger children. For your middle to high school teenagers, cut to the chase and tell them some of the things that can go wrong and have gone wrong with other kids around the world. Let them know that you're informed about the risks, you know how to handle technology, and that it's your job as a parent to set rules designed to protect them. Young to mature teenagers tend to feel that they're invincible. I remember that feeling well, but then again—we didn't have online predators when I was growing up.

- If they make a mistake or intentionally break the rules of your Internet agreement, keep a cool head. You may greatly dislike what they've done and be disappointed in them, but you're also supposed to be there for them when times get tough. That means keeping your temper in check and clearly explaining the risks of what they've done, and what the repercussions are.

- If they break the rules, stick to your guns and deliver the appropriate punishment, which may result in revoking some of their Internet privileges. A parent I know revoked her daughter's Internet rights when she became aware that her daughter had posted a page on MySpace, which was not allowed. Kids need consistency. Setting clear expectations with defined repercussions is only part of an Internet agreement with your child. Enforcing it is the other part.

- Never tell children that they're stupid as a result of what they've done. They may have done something foolish that puts them at risk, but words like *stupid* can have a different (and potentially devastating) impact.

ADVICE FROM THE PROS (CHILD PSYCHOLOGISTS)

I'm not a child psychologist or psychiatrist and wouldn't think of giving out advice to parents from their perspective. If parents are having difficulties talking to their children about issues, potential harms, or problems associated with the Internet or any other issue for that matter, there are always alternatives to ignoring the problem. Many professionals can help, including law enforcement, school counselors, social workers, family, friends, and, yes, child psychologists and psychiatrists. The Internet can be a great resource when looking for assistance. Use it and get some help from a professional if you sense that your child is in harm's way, involved in risky behavior, not listening, or displaying behavior that isn't consistent or condoned.

I asked Dr. Sam Hackworth, a private practice psychologist and CEO/founder of AskaChildPsychologist.com for some additional advice on how to get through to kids today at various ages in development. The following questions and answers are provided to give parents some additional help and advice from the perspective of a professional doctor.

Question: To what level can children comprehend the risks of going online (sexual predators, graphic pornography, hate materials, violence, kidnapping, etc.) at various age groups (category 1, elementary school; category 2, middle school; category 3, high school)?

Dr. Hackworth: Elementary school (ages 8–11): Very little understanding of online risks, and fleeting at that. Middle school (ages 12–14): Very limited understanding still, and very naive about it. High school (ages 15–18): Limited true comprehension, still with ongoing naiveté and tendency to "forget" the risks impulsively.

Q2: Why?

Dr. Hackworth: The youngest group, ages 8–11, typically don't think at all about what's on the Internet other than what is on the screen right in front of them. Faceless predators or criminals, down the street or around the globe, usually wouldn't cross their minds unless their parents or the news media told them about such possibilities—even then, I doubt that most kids this age would "remember" the risks without constant reminders. The middle school group, in my clinical experience, barely seems to get it. This age group can talk more about the risks and seem to know some real examples of things gone wrong, but they are very naive and expect that nothing could happen to them. They also very easily forget the basics about security, giving out personal information left and right. The high school group does tend to understand the risks to a more comforting level, but even then that varies widely across teens. Some in high school are vigilant and relatively mature, and try to be safe; others routinely operate just as the middle schoolers do—with great naiveté and immaturity. In my clinical experience, if anyone expresses great attraction or interest in any way to a certain subset of high schoolers, then that portion of them will "slip" and do something stupid on the Internet sometime.

Q3: If a child is physically or emotionally harmed as a result of an Internet-related event, how long does it take to complete a healing process?

Dr. Hackworth: That depends on too many variables to really answer. Can be from a short period to years long. If it's from a face-to-face event and involving anything physical, the healing could take years.

Q4: In your opinion, can many online/Internet-related crimes against children be prevented?

Dr. Hackworth: Yes.

Q5: How so?

Dr. Hackworth: By parents repeatedly educating and reeducating their children on the risks and how to be safer. And by monitoring what their children are doing and asking questions about their Internet experiences and contacts. One of the biggest things I think parents can do is continually drive home the fact that anyone could be up to anything on the Internet, telephone, and so on, and that their children should assume anything is possible. Remind them that letting their guard down would be like routinely forgetting to lock the doors at night. I think they know that somewhere in the world (again, down the street or around the globe) there are lots of people who would come in and commit criminal acts if they knew they had the opportunity.

Q6: What recommendations can you give parents regarding how to talk to their children about the risks of using the Internet?

Dr. Hackworth: (1) Even the most honest, responsible, and mature child or teen needs clear expectations about Internet use. Tell them exactly what you expect and exactly what the consequences will be for following through or not. (2) Be straightforward and frank about risks and dangers of putting oneself out there in the world via the Internet. The older they get, the less benefit to anyone to mince words. (3) Teach your child or teen to assume nothing on the Internet—to remember that anything is possible from anyone they (and you) don't know firsthand. (4) Talk with them regularly and frequently, keeping in mind that from elementary through high school a certain degree of repetition is necessary to learn most things. (5) Let them know they can talk with you about anything at any time.[3]

RECOMMENDATIONS

Parents today can make a difference in their children's life and improve their safety if they make an effort. Some adults are scared of technology, and many simply don't know where to begin to make the Internet safer for their children. This book provides parents and teachers with the tools and the road map to get it done.

I offer the Smith Safety Road Map (Figure 11.1), which is an eight-step approach to making your child's experiences on the Internet fun, educational, and safe. The roadmap summarizes some of the major steps and recommendations put forth in this book. Parents and guardians that follow the instructions and the more detailed recommendations within each chapter by age category will greatly reduce the risk of harm to their children. I close with the following recommendations.

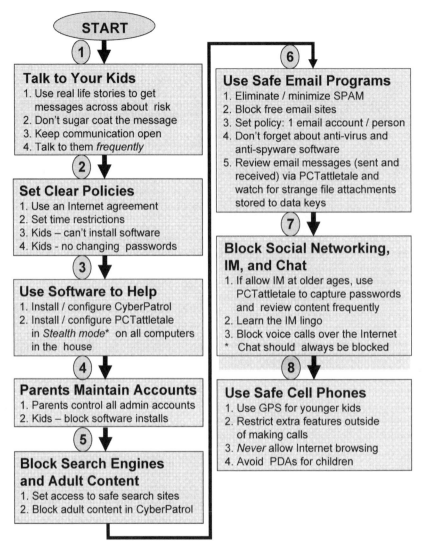

START

1 Talk to Your Kids
1. Use real life stories to get messages across about risk
2. Don't sugar coat the message
3. Keep communication open
4. Talk to them *frequently*

2 Set Clear Policies
1. Use an Internet agreement
2. Set time restrictions
3. Kids – can't install software
4. Kids - no changing passwords

3 Use Software to Help
1. Install / configure CyberPatrol
2. Install / configure PCTattletale in *Stealth mode** on all computers in the house

4 Parents Maintain Accounts
1. Parents control all admin accounts
2. Kids – block software installs

5 Block Search Engines and Adult Content
1. Set access to safe search sites
2. Block adult content in CyberPatrol

6 Use Safe Email Programs
1. Eliminate / minimize SPAM
2. Block free email sites
3. Set policy: 1 email account / person
4. Don't forget about anti-virus and anti-spyware software
5. Review email messages (sent and received) via PCTattletale and watch for strange file attachments stored to data keys

7 Block Social Networking, IM, and Chat
1. If allow IM at older ages, use PCTattletale to capture passwords and review content frequently
2. Learn the IM lingo
3. Block voice calls over the Internet
* Chat should always be blocked

8 Use Safe Cell Phones
1. Use GPS for younger kids
2. Restrict extra features outside of making calls
3. *Never* allow Internet browsing
4. Avoid PDAs for children

Figure 11.1 The Smith Safety Road Map

- Get up to speed on basic Internet and related technology and stay educated as the technology changes. Treat your knowledge of the Internet like a job—you must always be learning something new to stay ahead and keep competitive.
- Follow the road map outlined in this book. It's easy to do, given the types of technology recommended if you follow the steps, and it will help keep your kids safer.
- Be a technology-savvy parent. Don't make excuses when it comes to keeping your children safe on the Internet.
- The Internet is a really great place, but it's not always safe for children. Don't let kids roam loose. Set clear expectations and use Internet agreements to seal the deal regarding what behavior is acceptable and what's not.
- Set time restrictions for your children when accessing the Internet. Watch out for excessive time spent late at night on their computers. It may be a sign that they're talking to the strangers or accessing content and tools they shouldn't be.
- Use software to help protect your children on the Internet. Parents couldn't possibly protect their kids without the kinds of software like CyberPatrol and PC Tattletale. These programs are designed to make protection easier, especially when used together.
- Don't deprive your children of the Internet entirely. If used appropriately, it can be a great resource.
- Educating your kids is more than just talking about protecting them against the risks of the Internet. Education is about teaching them helpful facts, materials, and life lessons. Technology and the Internet can be an important tool in doing so. Don't leave educating your children to their teachers alone. Educators are important, but at the end of the day, it's a parent's job to raise their children in a safe and nurturing environment.
- If you become aware or suspect that your child has been harmed or abused as a result of using the Internet, call a professional for assistance. Here are some important numbers.

  1. Childhelp USA National Hotline (800) 4-A-CHILD (TDD 800-2-A-CHILD)
  2. National Center for Missing and Exploited Children, (800) 843-5678 (TDD 800-826-7653)
  3. National Children's Alliance, (800) 239-9950

- Never give up.

Notes

Chapter 1

1. DP-1, Profile of General Demographic Characteristics: 2000, U.S. Census, available online at factfinder.census.gov (accessed August 28, 2006).

2. Ibid.

3. Teen Internet Safety Study, Cox Communications and NCMEC, available online at www.netsmartz.org/safety/statistics.htm (accessed July 24, 2006).

4. Ibid.

5. Ibid.

6. Ibid.

7. "ARPA-DARPA: The History of the Name," U.S. Defense Advanced Research Projects Agency, available online at www.darpa.mil/body/arpa_darpa.html (accessed August 28, 2006).

8. Ibid.

9. "A Brief History of the Internet," *Internet Society*, available online at www.isoc.org/internet/history/brief.shtml (accessed August 28, 2006).

10. Ibid.

11. Ibid.

12. Ibid.

13. Ibid.

14. Ibid.

15. Ibid.

16. Ibid.

17. Wayne Rash, "Net Neutrality Advocates Face Off," *eWeek Magazine* (July 24, 2006), p. 20.

18. Kim Hart, "Center Opens to Train New Web Protocol Users," *Washington Post*, September 14, 2006, p. D4.

19. Ibid.

20. "Commodity Computing," Wikipedia, available online at en.wikipedia.org/wiki/Commodity_computing (accessed September 4, 2006).

21. Ibid.

22. "Computer History: History of Microsoft Windows," ComputerHope, available online at www.computerhope.com/history/windows.htm (accessed September 4, 2006).

23. Ibid.

24. "What Are CERN's Greatest Achievements: History of the WWW," CERN, available online at public.web.cern.ch/public/Content/Chapters/AboutCERN/Achievements/WorldWideWeb/WebHistory/WebHistory-en.html (accessed September 4, 2006).

25. "The History of HTML," About, available online at inventors.about.com/library/inventors/blhtml.htm (accessed September 4, 2006).

26. "Web Inventor Wins $1.23 Million Award," MSNBC, available online at msnbc.msn.com/id/4744554 (accessed September 4, 2006).

27. "What Are CERN's Greatest Achievements."

28. Ibid.

29. Ibid.

30. Ibid.

31. Ibid.

32. "Happy Birthday, Altavista!" SearchEngineWatch.com (December 18, 2002), available online at searchenginewatch.com/showPage.html?page=2161421 (accessed September 11, 2006).

33. Company overview, Google, available online at www.google.com/intl/en/corporate/index.html (accessed September 11, 2006).

34. Company profile, Research in Motion, available online at www.rim.com/company/index.shtml (accessed September 11, 2006).

35. "Neutral Net: A Battle for Control of the Web," *Wall Street Journal*, June 24–25, 2006, p. A9.

36. "Worldwide Internet Users Top 1 Billion in 2005," Computer Industry Almanac, available online at www.c-i-a.com/pr0106.htm (accessed September 11, 2006).

37. Ibid.

38. Ibid.

39. Pam Tobey, "Trend Lines: Digital Divide," *Washington Post*, September 10, 2006, p. A2.

40. Ibid.

41. Ibid.

Chapter 3

1. Amanda Lenhart, Mary Madden, Lee Rainie, Pew Internet and American Life Project, *Teens and the Internet—Findings Submitted to the House Subcommittee on Telecommunications and the Internet*, July 11, 2006, p. 2. www.pewinternet.org.

2. Ibid., p. 5.

3. Ibid.

4. Ibid.

5. Ibid., p. 2.

6. "125 Arrested in Child Porn Roundup," CNN.com, available online at www.cnn.com/2006/US/10/18/child.porn/index.html (accessed October 19, 2006).

7. Ibid.

8. Ibid.

9. Ibid.

10. "A Secret Life," *Newsweek* (October 16, 2006), p. 33.

11. Ibid.

12. Ibid.

13. Ibid.

14. Ibid., p. 34.

15. "Ads to Warn Teens about Web Crimes," *USA Today*, August 22, 2006, p. 5A.

16. Ibid.

17. Dana Bash, "Congressman Quits after Messages Sent to Teens Found," CNN.com, September 30, 2006, available online at www.cnn.com/2006/POLITICS/09/29/congressman.e.mails/index.html (accessed October 1, 2006).

18. Amy Satkofsky, "In the Web," Pennlive.com, *Express-Times*, February 25, 2004, available online at www.pennlive.com/specialprojects/expresstimes/index.ssf?/news/expresstimes/stories/molesters4_mainbar.html (accessed November 29, 2006).

19. Excerpts from Panorama BBC1, Canadian Children Rights Council, October 6, 1997, available online at www.canadiancrc.com/female_sexual_predators_awareness.htm (accessed November 30, 2006).

20. Frederick Mathews, "The Invisible Boy: Revisioning the Victimization of Male Children and Teens 1996," 1996, available online at www.canadiancrc.com/The_Invisible_Boy_Report.htm (accessed November 30, 2006).

21. Ibid.

22. "The Ultimate Taboo: Child Sexual Abuse by Women," BBC World Service, October 6, 1997, available online at www.canadiancrc.com/articles/BBC_Child_sexual_abuse_by_women_06OCT97.htm (accessed November 30, 2006).

23. Satkofsky, "In the Web."

24. "Sexual Abuse of Children," Prevent Child Abuse, available online at www.ridalaskaofchildabuse.org/PCAA_CSA.html (accessed November 30, 2006).

25. Senator Leo T. Foley, "S.F. No. 2873—Solicitation of a Child to Engage in Sexual Conduct," State of Minnesota Senate, February 23, 2000, available online at www.senate.leg.state.mn.us/departments/scr/billsumm/1999–2000/SF2873.HTM (accessed November 30, 2006).

26. Jen Stadler, "Online Child Molesters," Netsmartz, available online at www.netsmartz.org/news/onlinemolesters.htm (accessed November 20, 2006).

27. "About Us," Netsmartz Workshop, available online at www.netsmartz.org/overview/aboutus.htm (accessed December 2, 2006).

28. "Statistics—Teen Internet Safety Study," Netsmartz, available online at www.netsmartz.org/safety/statistics.htm (accessed July 24, 2006).

29. "National Mandate and Mission," National Center for Missing and Exploited Children, available online at www.missingkids.com/missingkids/servlet/PageServlet?LanguageCountry=en_US&PageId=1866 (accessed December 3, 2006).

30. Ibid.

31. David Finkelhor, Kimberly J. Mitchell, and Janis Wolak, "Online Victimization: A Report on the Nation's Youth," National Center for Missing and Exploited Children, June 2000, pp. 9, 15, and 16.

32. Ibid.

33. Kimberly Mitchell, David Finkelhor, and Janis Wolak, "The Exposure of Youth to Unwanted Sexual Material on the Internet: A National Survey of Risk, Impact, and Prevention," *Youth & Society*, 2003, 34(3): 330–58, available online at www.unh.edu/ccrc/pdf/Exposure_risk.pdf (accessed September 12, 2006).

34. Ketchum Global Research Network, "Parents' Internet Monitoring Study," National Center for Missing and Exploited Children, Cox Communications, and Netsmartz, 2005, available online at www.netsmartz.org/pdf/takechargestudy.pdf (accessed December 18, 2006).

35. Children's Online Privacy Protection Act of 1998, U.S. Federal Trade Commission, 1998, available online at www.ftc.gov/ogc/coppa1.htm (accessed September 8, 2006).

36. Children's Internet Protection Act, U.S. Federal Communications Commission, 2000, available online at www.fcc.gov/cgb/consumerfacts/cipa.html (accessed December 18, 2006).

Chapter 4

1. Amy Satkofsky, "Technology Provides Anonymous Access to Children," *Express-Times* (February 25, 2004), available online at www.pennlive.com/specialprojects/expresstimes/index.ssf?/news/expresstimes/stories/molesters4_mainbar.html (accessed November 20, 2006).

2. Ibid.

3. "Kacie René Woody," Kacie Woody Foundation, available online at home.alltel.net/rkw/kaciewoody_a.html (accessed November 20, 2006).

4. Ibid.

5. Ibid.

6. Christine Loftus, "Teen Murdered by Man She Met in Chatroom," Netsmartz, available online at www.netsmartz.org/news/dec02–02.htm (accessed November 20, 2006).

7. "Kacie René Woody."

8. Ibid.

9. "Help to Halt Online Predators," CBS News, May 8, 2003, available online at www.cbsnews.com/stories/2003/05/07/earlyshow/living/parenting/main552841.shtml (accessed November 20, 2006).

10. Ibid.

11. Ibid.

12. Jen Stadler, "Online Child Molesters," Netsmartz, available online at www.netsmartz.org/news/onlinemolesters.htm (accessed November 20, 2006).

13. Ibid.

14. Christine Loftus, "12-Year-Old Girl Back Home after Ordeal," Netsmartz, available online at www.netsmartz.org/news/jul03–03.htm (accessed November 20, 2006).

15. Ibid.

16. Ibid.

17. Ibid.

18. Ibid.

19. Ibid.

20. Stadler, "Online Child Molesters."

21. Ibid.

22. Ibid.

23. Ibid.

24. Ibid.

25. "Three Arrested in Internet Kidnapping, Assault Case," USAToday.com, August 14, 2001, available online at www.usatoday.com/news/nation/2001/08/14/netcrime.htm (accessed November 20, 2006).

26. Ibid.

27. Ibid.

28. Ibid.

29. "Life Jail for Minister Who Lured Boys via Internet," *The News* (Portsmouth, UK), July 28, 2006, available online at www.portsmouthtoday.co.uk/ViewArticle2.aspx? SectionID=455&ArticleID=1660093 (accessed November 22, 2006).

30. Ibid.

31. Ibid.

32. Ibid.

33. Ibid.

34. Hilary Hylton, "Another Suit in the MySpace Case?" Time.com, June 22, 2006, available online at www.time.com/time/nation/article/0,8599,1207043,00.html (accessed November 22, 2006).

35. Ibid.

36. Ibid.

37. Ibid.

38. "Man Indicted for Having Sex with Two Boys He Met on the Internet," *Daily News Journal*, July 14, 2006, available online at http://observer.guardian.co.uk/world/ story/0,,1833433,00.html (accessed July 30, 2006).

39. "Police Uncover the Depraved World of Supalover666," Buzzle, available online at www.buzzle.com/editorials/7–29-2006–103877.asp (accessed November 27, 2006).

40. Ibid.

41. Ibid.

42. Ibid.

43. Ibid.

44. Ibid.

45. Ibid.

46. Ibid.

47. Ibid.

48. Ibid.

49. Ibid.

50. "Child Rape Suspect Used Internet to Lure Girls," *The Local—Sweden's News in*

English, March 29, 2006, available online at www.thelocal.se/article.php?ID=3408&
date=20060329 (accessed November 27, 2006).

51. Ibid.

52. Ibid.

53. Ibid.

54. Wendy Leonard, "Man Charged with Rape of Child," *Deseret News*, Utah News,
April 11, 2006, available online at deseretnews.com/dn/view/0,1249,635198653,00.html
(accessed November 27, 2006).

55. Ibid.

56. Wendy Leonard, "Orem Man Admits to Phone Porn," *Deseret News*, Utah News,
April 28, 2006, available online at deseretnews.com/dn/view/0,1249,635203179,00.html
(accessed November 27, 2006).

57. Ibid.

58. Ibid.

59. Eliza Barlow, "Break Came from Two Girls," *Edmonton Sun*, July 29, 2006, available online at www.edmontonsun.com/News/Edmonton/2006/07/29/1708968-sun.html
(accessed November 27, 2006).

60. Ibid.

61. Ibid.

62. Ibid.

63. Ibid.

64. Leila Fujimori, "Police Arrest Man Found in Teen's Bed," StarBulletin (Honolulu), February 15, 2006, available online at starbulletin.com/2006/02/15/news/story05.
html (accessed November 27, 2006).

65. Ibid.

66. Ibid.

67. "Waikiki Man Arrested for Allegedly Sexually Assaulting Teen Girl," KHNL,
March 14, 2006, available online at www.khnl.com/Global/story.asp?S=4627504 (accessed November 27, 2006).

68. Ibid.

69. Ibid.

70. Ibid.

71. "Internet Predator Sentenced for Seducing League City Girl," KHOU, August 4,
2006, available online at www.khou.com/news/local/galveston/stories/khou060804_
mh_minorsexsentence.21ba6de.html (accessed November 27, 2006).

72. Ibid.

73. Ibid.

74. "RadioShack Director Quits; Faces Child Porn Charges," CNNMoney.com, November 2, 2006, available online at money.cnn.com/2006/11/02/news/companies/bc.re
tail.radioshack.reut/index.htm (accessed November 3, 2006).

75. Tony Blais, "Mother Pleads Guilty for Molesting Son for Master," *Ottawa Sun*,
May 2, 2006, available online at www.canadiancrc.com/articles/Ottawa_Sun_Mother_
guilty_molesting%20_son_02MAY06.htm (accessed November 30, 2006).

76. Ibid.

77. Ibid.

Chapter 5

1. Jonathan Zittrain, "Can the Internet Survive Filtering?" CNET News, July 23, 2002, available online at news.com.com/2102–1071_3–945690.html?tag=st.util.print (accessed September 8, 2006).

2. Ibid.

3. "Government Study: Web 1 Percent Porn," CNN.com, November 16, 2006, available online at http://www.forumopolis.com/showthread.php?t=37593 (accessed November 16, 2006).

4. Ibid.

5. Ibid.

6. Ibid.

7. Ibid.

8. Jessica E. Vascellaro and Anjali Athavaley, "Foley Scandal Turns Parents into Web Sleuths," *Wall Street Journal*, October 18, 2006, p. D1.

9. "Government Study: Web 1 Percent Porn."

Chapter 6

1. "Web Reaches New Milestone: 100 Million Sites," CNN.com, November 1, 2006, available online at www.cnn.com/2006/TECH/internet/11/01/100millionwebsites/index.html (accessed November 1, 2006).

2. Ibid.

3. Ibid.

4. Ibid.

5. "Why on Earth Does the World Need Another Search Engine," *Wall Street Journal*, October 27, 2006, p. B3.

6. "Harvard Criticizes Google's Adult Content Filter," Search Engine Watch, April 16, 2006, available online at searchenginewatch.com/showPage.html?page=2191611 (accessed October 3, 2006).

7. Danny Sullivan, "Hitwise Search Engine Ratings," Search Engine Watch, August 23, 2006, available online at searchenginewatch.com/showPage.html?page=3099931 (accessed January 2, 2007).

8. Danny Sullivan, "Search Engine Sizes," Search Engine Watch, January 20, 2005, available online at searchenginewatch.com/showPage.html?page=2156481 (accessed January 2, 2007).

9. Ibid.

10. Ibid.

11. Danny Sullivan, "Kids Search Engines," Search Engine Watch, April 4, 2005, available online at searchenginewatch.com/showPage.html?page=2156191 (accessed October 3, 2007).

12. Ibid.

13. Testimony of Dr. Mary Anne Layden, "The Science Behind Pornography Addiction," U.S. Senate Hearings, Science, Technology, and Space hearing, November 18, 2004, available online at commerce.senate.gov/hearings/testimony.cfm?id=1343&wit_id=3912 (accessed January 1, 2007).

14. Ibid.

15. Ibid.

16. Ibid.

17. Ibid.

18. "Teen Testimonials on Internet Porn and Recovery," Protect Kids, available online at www.protectkids.com/effects/teentestimonials.htm (accessed January 11, 2007).

19. Ibid.

20. Ibid.

21. Yuki Noguchi, "Xanga to Pay $1 Million in Children's Privacy Case," *Washington Post*, September 8, 2006, p. D5.

22. Amanda Lenhart and Susannah Fox, "A Blogger Portrait," Pew Research Center, July 19, 2006, available online at pewresearch.org/pubs/236/a-blogger-portrait (accessed November 5, 2006).

23. Ibid.

24. Ibid.

25. Vauhini Vara, "MySpace Has Large Circle of Friends, But Rivals' Cliques Are Growing Too," *Wall Street Journal*, October 2, 2006, p. B1.

26. Ibid.

27. "Facebook to Open Its Membership Eligibility," *Wall Street Journal*, September 13, 2006, p. D4.

28. "Networking Sites Fight for Fickle Teen Users," *Washington Post*, October 29, 2006, p. A11.

29. Steve Israel, "Strangers in MySpace," Recordonline, February 12, 2006, available online at archive.recordonline.com/archive/2006/02/12/myspace.html (accessed January 9, 2007).

30. Ibid.

31. "Fear and Loathing on MySpace," *Washington Post*, June 27, 2006, available online at www.washingtonpost.com/wp-dyn/content/article/2006/06/27/AR2006062700709.html (accessed July 21, 2006).

32. Ibid.

33. "NJ Students Suspended over Web Postings," 1010wins, available online at www.1010wins.com/pages/24851.php? (accessed January 29, 2007).

34. Ibid.

35. May Wong, "Online Video Boom Raises Risks, Concerns," *Washington Post*, July 9, 2006, available online at www.washingtonpost.com/wp-dyn/content/article/2006/07/09/AR2006070900346.html (accessed July 21, 2006).

36. Ibid.

37. Ibid.

38. "YouTube Blocked in Much of Brazil," CNN.com, January 8, 2007, available online at cnn.com/2007/WORLD/americas/01/08/youtube.brazil.ap/index.html (accessed January 9, 2007).

39. Ibid.

Chapter 7

1. Heinz Tschabitscher, "Top 10 Free Email Services," About, available online at email.about.com/cs/freemailreviews/tp/free_email.htm (accessed January 11, 2007).

2. "Types of Email Service," Emailaddresses, available online at www.emailaddresses.com/guide_types.htm (accessed January 11, 2007).

3. Heinz Tschabitscher, "Top 10 Free Email Programs for Windows," About, available online at email.about.com/od/windowsemailclients/tp/free_email_prog.htm (accessed January 11, 2007).

4. Resource Center, Postini.com, available online at www.postini.com/stats (accessed January 11, 2007).

5. Ibid.

6. Ibid.

7. Ibid.

Chapter 9

1. "By the Numbers," *eWeek Magazine*, February 5, 2007, p. 31.

2. Tracy V. Wilson, "How GPS Phones Work," HowStuffWorks, available online at electronics.howstuffworks.com/gps-phone.htm (accessed February 9, 2007).

3. Ibid.

4. Ibid.

5. Rob Pegoraro, "Watch Out, Kids: With GPS Phones, Big Mother Is Watching," *Washington Post*, April 19, 2006, p. D1, available online at www.washingtonpost.com/wp-dyn/content/article/2006/04/18/AR2006041801604.html (accessed February 9, 2007).

6. Wilson, "How GPS Phones Work."

7. Ibid.

8. Ibid.

9. Ibid.

10. WatchZone Web site, available online at www.watchzone.com/cgi-bin/watchzone.filereader?45cfd6db00046c1c27430a801252064a+EN/catalogs/3412 (accessed February 11, 2007).

11. Ibid.

12. "Learn Kids Codes for Instant Messages," Wesh, May 5, 2006, available online at www.wesh.com/print/4454738/detail.html (accessed October 27, 2006).

Chapter 10

1. Susan Crawford, quoted in "Imagining the Internet: A History and Forecast," Elon University/Pew Internet Project, 2004 Survey, Prediction on Social Networks, available online at www.elon.edu/e-web/predictions/expertsurveys/2004_socialnetworks.xhtml (accessed February 12, 2007).

2. "Imagining the Internet."

3. Dr. William Webb, "Predictions for the Mobile Future," BBCNews, January 10, 2007, available online at news.bbc.co.uk/1/hi/technology/6232243.stm (accessed January 25, 2007).

4. A. Halavais, quoted in "Imagining the Internet."

5. "Imagining the Internet."

Chapter 11

1. "10 Tips for Talking with Kids about Tough Issues," Talk with Your Kids, available online at www.talkingwithkids.org/first.html (accessed February 13, 2007).

2. Ibid.

3. Interview with Dr. Sam Hackworth, January 22, 2007, via completion of a survey.

Bibliography

Journal Articles

"A Secret Life," *Newsweek* (October 16, 2006), pp. 33–34.

"By the Numbers," *eWeek Magazine* (February 5, 2007), p. 31.

Finkelhor, David, Kimberly J. Mitchell, and Janis Wolak. "Online Victimization: A Report on the Nation's Youth," National Center for Missing and Exploited Children, June 2000.

Lenhart, Amanda, Mary Madden, and Lee Rainie. Pew Internet and American Life Project, *Teens and the Internet—Findings Submitted to the House Subcommittee on Telecommunications and the Internet*, July 11, 2006, pp. 2–5.

Rash, Wayne. "Net Neutrality Advocates Face Off," *eWeek Magazine* (July 24, 2006), p. 20.

Newspaper Articles

"Ads to Warn Teens about Web Crimes," *USA Today*, August 22, 2006, p. 5A.

"Facebook to Open Its Membership Eligibility," *Wall Street Journal*, September 13, 2006, p. D4.

Hart, Kim. "Center Opens to Train New Web Protocol Users," *Washington Post*, September 14, 2006, p. D4.

"Networking Sites Fight for Fickle Teen Users," *Washington Post*, October 29, 2006, p. A11.

"Neutral Net: A Battle for Control of the Web," *Wall Street Journal*, June 24–25, 2006, p. A9.

Noguchi, Yuki. "Xanga to Pay $1 Million in Children's Privacy Case," *Washington Post*, September 8, 2006, p. D5.

Tobey, Pam. "Trend Lines: Digital Divide," *Washington Post*, September 10, 2006, p. A2.

Vara, Vauhini. "MySpace Has Large Circle of Friends, But Rivals' Cliques Are Growing Too," *Wall Street Journal*, October 2, 2006, p. B1.

Vascellaro. Jessica E. and Anjali Athavaley. "Foley Scandal Turns Parents Into Web Sleuths," The Wall Street Journal, October 18, 2006, p. D1.

"Why on Earth Does the World Need Another Search Engine," *Wall Street Journal*, October 27, 2006, p. B3.

Interviews

Interview with Dr. Sam Hackworth, January 22, 2007, via completion of a survey.

Web survey of parents about how they protect their children online; 100 surveys completed and used in the analysis. Survey designed by author on September 1, 2006.

Web Articles

"10 Tips for Talking with Kids about Tough Issues," Talking With Kids, available online at www.talkingwithkids.org/first.html (accessed February 13, 2007).

"125 Arrested in Child Porn Roundup," CNN, available online at www.cnn.com/2006/US/10/18/child.porn/index.html (accessed October 19, 2006).

"A Brief History of the Internet," Internet Society, available online at www.isoc.org/internet/history/brief.shtml (accessed August 28, 2006).

"About Us," Netsmartz Workshop, available online at www.netsmartz.org/overview/aboutus.htm (accessed December 2, 2006).

Barlow, Eliza. "Break Came from Two Girls," *Edmonton Sun*, July 29, 2006, available online at www.edmontonsun.com/News/Edmonton/2006/07/29/1708968-sun.html (accessed November 27, 2006).

Bash, Dana. "Congressman Quits after Messages Sent to Teens Found," CNN, September 30, 2006, available online at www.cnn.com/2006/POLITICS/09/29/congressman.e.mails/index.html (accessed October 1, 2006).

Blais, Tony. "Mother Pleads Guilty for Molesting Son for Master." *Ottawa Sun*, May 2, 2006, available online at www.canadiancrc.com/articles/Ottawa_Sun_Mother_guilty_molesting%20_son_02MAY06.htm (accessed November 30, 2006).

"Child Rape Suspect Used Internet to Lure Girls," *The Local*--Sweden's News in English, March 29, 2006, available online at www.thelocal.se/article.php?ID=3408&date=20060329 (accessed November 27, 2006.

"Children's Internet Protection Act," U.S. Federal Communications Commission, 2000, available online at www.fcc.gov/cgb/consumerfacts/cipa.html (accessed December 18, 2006).

"Children's Online Privacy Protection Act of 1998," U.S. Federal Trade Commission, 1998, available online at www.ftc.gov/ogc/coppa1.htm (accessed September 8, 2006).

"Commodity Computing," Wikipedia, available online at en.wikipedia.org/wiki/Commodity_computing (accessed September 4, 2006).

"Computer History: History of Microsoft Windows," Computer Hope, available online at www.computerhope.com/history/windows.htm (accessed September 4, 2006).

Excerpts from Panorama BBC1, Canadian Children Rights Council, October 6, 1997, available online at www.canadiancrc.com/female_sexual_predators_awareness.htm (accessed November 30, 2006).

"Fear and Loathing on MySpace," *Washington Post*, June 27, 2006, available online at www.washingtonpost.com/wp-dyn/content/article/2006/06/27/AR2006062700709_2.html (accessed July 21, 2006).

Foley, Senator Leo T. "S.F. No. 2873—Solicitation of a Child to Engage in Sexual Conduct," State of Minnesota Senate, February 23, 2000, available online at www.senate.leg.state.mn.us/departments/scr/billsumm/1999–2000/SF2873.HTM (accessed November 30, 2006).

Fujimori, Leila. "Police Arrest Man Found in Teen's Bed," *Star Bulletin*, February 15, 2006, available online at starbulletin.com/2006/02/15/news/story05.html (accessed November 27, 2006).

"Government Study: Web 1 Percent Porn," CNN.com, November 16, 2006, available online at www.cnn.com/2006/TECH/internet/11/15/internet.blocking.ap/index.html (accessed November 16, 2006).

"Happy Birthday, Altavista!" Search Engine Watch, December 18, 2002, available online at searchenginewatch.com/showPage.html?page=2161421 (accessed September 11, 2006).

"Harvard Criticizes Google's Adult Content Filter," Search Engine Watch, April 16, 2006, available online at earchenginewatch.com/showPage.html?page=2191611 (accessed October 3, 2006).

"Help to Halt Online Predators," CBS News, May 8, 2003, available online at www.cbsnews.com/stories/2003/05/07/earlyshow/living/parenting/main552841.shtml (accessed November 20, 2006).

"The History of HTML," About, available online at inventors.about.com/library/inventors/blhtml.htm (accessed September 4, 2006).

Hylton, Hilary. "Another Suit in the MySpace Case," Time.com, June 22, 2006, available online at www.time.com/time/nation/article/0,8599,1207043,00.html (accessed November 22, 2006).

"Imagining the Internet: A History and Forecast," Elon University/Pew Internet Project, The 2004 Survey. Prediction on social networks available online at www.elon.edu/-web/predictions/expertsurveys/2004_socialnetworks.xhtml; Prediction on families available online at www.elon.edu/e-web/predictions/expertsurveys/2004_families.xhtml; Prediction about how people go online available online at www.elon.edu/e-web/predictions/expertsurveys/2004_online.xhtml; Prediction on network infrastructure available online at www.elon.edu/predictions/q9.aspx (accessed February 12, 2007).

"Internet Predator Sentenced for Seducing League City Girl," KHOU, August 4, 2006, available online at www.khou.com/news/local/galveston/stories/khou060804_mh_minorsexsentence.21ba6de.html (accessed November 27, 2006).

Israel, Steve. "Strangers in MySpace," Recordonline, February 12, 2006, available online at archive.recordonline.com/archive/2006/02/12/myspace.html (accessed January 9, 2007).

"Learn Kids Codes for Instant Messages," Wesh, May 5, 2006, available online at www.wesh.com/print/4454738/detail.html (accessed October 27, 2006).

Lenhart, Amanda and Susannah Fox. "A Blogger Portrait," Pew Research Center, July 19, 2006, available online at pewresearch.org/reports/?ReportID=36 (accessed November 5, 2006).

Leonard, Wendy. "Man Charged with Rape of Child," *Deseret News*, Utah News, April 11, 2006, available online at deseretnews.com/dn/view/0,1249,635198653,00.html (accessed November 27, 2006).

Leonard, Wendy. "Orem man admits to phone porn," *Deseret News*, Utah News, April 28, 2006, available online at deseretnews.com/dn/view/0,1249,635203179,00.html (accessed November 27, 2006).

"Life Jail for Minister Who Lured Boys via Internet," *The News* (Portsmouth, UK), July 28, 2006, available online at www.portsmouthtoday.co.uk/ViewArticle2.aspx?SectionID=455&ArticleID=1660093 (accessed November 22, 2006).

Loftus, Christine. "12-Year-Old Girl Back Home after Ordeal," Netsmartz, available online at www.netsmartz.org/news/jul03–03.htm (accessed November 20, 2006).

Loftus, Christine. "Teen Murdered by Man She Met in Chatroom," Netsmartz, available online at www.netsmartz.org/news/dec02–02.htm (accessed November 20, 2006).

"Man Indicted for Having Sex with Two Boys He Met on the Internet," *Daily News Journal*, July 14, 2006, available online at dnj.midsouthnews.com/apps/pbcs.dll/article?AID=/20060714/NEWS01/60714002 (accessed July 17, 2006).

Mathews, Frederick. "The Invisible Boy: Revisioning the Victimization of Male Children and Teens 1996," 1996, available online at www.canadiancrc.com/The_Invisible_Boy_Report.htm (accessed November 30, 2006).

Mitchell, Kimberly, David Finkelhor, and Janis Wolak, "The Exposure of Youth to Unwanted Sexual Material on the Internet: A National Survey of Risk, Impact, and Prevention," *Youth & Society*, 2003, available online at www.unh.edu/ccrc/pdf/Exposure_risk.pdf (accessed September 12, 2006).

"National Mandate and Mission," National Center for Missing and Exploited Children, available online at www.missingkids.com/missingkids/servlet/PageServlet?LanguageCountry=en_US&PageId=1866 (accessed December 3, 2006).

"NJ Students Suspended over Web Postings," 1010wins, available online at www.1010wins.com/pages/24851.php? (accessed January 29, 2007).

"Online Victimization of Youth: Five Years Later," Cox Communications and NCMEC survey, available online at www.netsmartz.org/safety/statistics.htm (accessed July 24, 2006).

"Parents' Internet Monitoring Study," National Center for Missing and Exploited Children and Cox Communications, 2005, available online at www.netsmartz.org/pdf/takechargestudy.pdf (accessed December 18, 2006).

Pegoraro, Rob. "Watch Out, Kids: With GPS Phones, Big Mother Is Watching," *Washington Post*, April 19, 2006, available online at www.washingtonpost.com/wp-dyn/content/article/2006/04/18/AR2006041801604.html (accessed February 9, 2007).

"Police Uncover the Depraved World of Supalover666," Buzzle, available online at www.buzzle.com/editorials/7–29-2006–103877.asp (accessed November 27, 2006).

"Profile of General Demographic Characteristics: 2000," U.S. Census, available online at factfinder.census.gov

"RadioShack Director Quits; Faces Child Porn Charges," CNNMoney.com, November

2, 2006, available online at money.cnn.com/2006/11/02/news/companies/bc.retail. radioshack.reut/index.htm (accessed November 3, 2006).

Satkofsky, Amy. "In the Web," Pennlive, *Express-Times*, February 25, 2004, available online at www.pennlive.com/specialprojects/expresstimes/index.ssf?/news/express-times/stories/molesters4_mainbar.html (accessed November 29, 2006).

Satkofsky, Amy. "Technology Provides Anonymous Access to Children," *Express-Times*, February 25, 2004, available online at www.pennlive.com/specialprojects/expresstimes/index.ssf?/news/expresstimes/stories/molesters4_mainbar.html (accessed November 20, 2006).

"The Science behind Pornography Addition," testimony of Dr. Mary Anne Layden, U.S. Senate Hearings, Science, Technology, and Space hearing, November 18, 2004, available online at commerce.senate.gov/hearings/testimony.cfm?id=1343&wit_id=3912 (accessed January 1, 2007).

"Sexual Abuse of Children," Prevent Child Abuse, available online at www.ridalaskaof-childabuse.org/PCAA_CSA.html (accessed November 30, 2006).

Stadler, Jen. "Online Child Molesters," Netsmartz, available online at www.netsmartz.org/news/onlinemolesters.htm (accessed November 20, 2006).

"Statistics—Teen Internet Safety Study," Netsmartz, available online at www.netsmartz.org/safety/statistics.htm (accessed July 24, 2006).

Sullivan, Danny. "Hitwise Search Engine Ratings," Search Engine Watch, August 23, 2006, available online at searchenginewatch.com/showPage.html?page=3099931 (accessed January 2, 2007).

Sullivan, Danny. "Kids Search Engines," Search Engine Watch, April 4, 2005, available online at searchenginewatch.com/showPage.html?page=2156191 (accessed October 3, 2007).

Sullivan, Danny. "Search Engine Sizes," Search Engine Watch, January 20, 2005, available online at searchenginewatch.com/showPage.html?page=2156481 (accessed January 2, 2007).

"Teen Testimonials on Internet Porn and Recovery," Protect Kids. available online at www.protectkids.com/effects/teentestimonials.htm (accessed January 11, 2007).

"Three Arrested in Internet Kidnapping, Assault Case," *USAToday*, August 14, 2001, available online at www.usatoday.com/news/nation/2001/08/14/netcrime.htm (accessed November 20, 2006).

Tschabitscher, Heinz. "Top 10 Free Email Programs for Windows," About, available online at email.about.com/od/windowsemailclients/tp/free_email_prog.htm (accessed January 11, 2007).

Tschabitscher, Heinz. "Top 10 Free Email Services," About, available online at email.about.com/cs/freemailreviews/tp/free_email.htm (accessed January 11, 2007).

"Types of Email Service," Emailaddresses, available online at www.emailaddresses.com/guide_types.htm (accessed January 11, 2007).

"The Ultimate Taboo: Child Sexual Abuse by Women," BBC World Service, October 6, 1997, available online at www.canadiancrc.com/articles/BBC_Child_sexual_abuse_by_women_06OCT97.htm (accessed November 30, 2006).

"Waikiki Man Arrested for Allegedly Sexually Assaulting Teen Girl," KHNL, March 14, 2006, available online at www.khnl.com/Global/story.asp?S=4627504 (accessed November 27, 2006).

"Web Inventor Wins $1.23 Million Award," MSNBC, available online at msnbc.msn. com/id/4744554/ (accessed September 4, 2006).

"Web Reaches New milestone: 100 Million Sites," CNN.com, November 1, 2006, available online at www.cnn.com/2006/TECH/internet/11/01/100millionwebsites/index. html (accessed November 1, 2006).

Webb, William. "Predictions for the Mobile Future," BBCNews, January 10, 2007, available online at news.bbc.co.uk/1/hi/technology/6232243.stm (accessed January 25, 2007).

"What Are CERN's Greatest Achievements: History of the WWW," CERN, available online at public.web.cern.ch/public/Content/Chapters/AboutCERN/Achievements/ WorldWideWeb/WebHistory/WebHistory-en.html (accessed September 4, 2006).

Wilson, Tracy V. "How GPS Phones Work," HowStuffWorks, available online at electronics.howstuffworks.com/gps-phone.htm (accessed February 9, 2007).

Wong, May. "Online Video Boom Raises Risks, Concerns," *Washington Post*, July 9, 2006. available online at www.washingtonpost.com/wp-dyn/content/article/2006/07/ 09/AR2006070900346.html (accessed July 21, 2006).

"Worldwide Internet Users Top 1 Billion in 2005," Computer Industry Almanac, available online at www.c-i-a.com/pr0106.htm (accessed September 11, 2006).

"YouTube Blocked in Much of Brazil," CNN, January 8, 2007, available online at cnn. com/2007/WORLD/americas/01/08/youtube.brazil.ap/index.html (accessed January 9, 2007).

Zittrain, Jonathan. "Can the Internet Survive Filtering?" CNET News, July 23, 2002, available online at news.com.com/2102–1071_3–945690.html?tag=st.util.print (accessed September 8, 2006).

Index

ABOUT THE AUTHOR

GREGORY S. SMITH is Vice President and Chief Information Officer (CIO) of Information Technology at the World Wildlife Fund in Washington, D.C. and Adjunct Professor in the School of Professional Studies in Business and Education Graduate Programs at The Johns Hopkins University. He is an expert in the field of information technology with several technical articles and public speaking engagements to his credit. In addition, he is the author of *Straight to the Top: Becoming a World-Class CIO.*